A RIDE TO INDIA ACROSS PERSIA AND BALUCHISTÁN

First published 1891
This edition published by Lector House in 2023

ISBN: 978-93-5800-779-4

Lector House LLP
Registered Office: H. No. 96, Block C, Tomar Colony,
Burari, Delhi – 110084, India
info@lectorhouse.com
www.lectorhouse.com

A RIDE TO INDIA
ACROSS PERSIA AND BALUCHISTÁN

HARRY DE WINDT

2023

LECTOR HOUSE

LECTOR HOUSE LLP

IN THE DESERT: SUNRISE

A RIDE TO INDIA
ACROSS PERSIA AND BALUCHISTÁN

BY

HARRY DE WINDT, F.R.G.S.,

AUTHOR OF
"FROM PEKIN TO CALAIS BY LAND," ETC.

**WITH ILLUSTRATIONS
BY
HERBERT WALKER
FROM SKETCHES BY THE AUTHOR**

TO
AUDLEY LOVELL, ESQUIRE,
COLDSTREAM GUARDS,
THIS VOLUME
IS
DEDICATED.

CONTENTS

LIST OF ILLUSTRATIONS

Page

A RIDE TO INDIA.

CHAPTER I.

TIFLIS—BAKU.

"Ceci non!"

A spacious apartment, its polished *parquet* strewn with white bearskins and the thickest and softest of Persian rugs; its panelled walls hung with Oriental tapestries, costly daggers, pistols, and shields of barbaric, but beautiful, workmanship, glistening with gold and silver. Every detail of the room denotes the artistic taste of the owner. Inlaid tables and Japanese cabinets are littered with priceless porcelain and *cloisonné,* old silver, and diamond-set miniatures; the low divans are heaped with cushions of deep-tinted satin and gold; heavy violet plush curtains drape the windows; while huge palms, hothouse plants, and bunches of sweet-smelling Russian violets occupy every available nook and corner. The pinewood fire flashes fitfully on a masterpiece of Vereschágin's, which stands on an easel by the hearth, and the massive gold "ikon,"[1] encrusted with diamonds and precious stones, in the corner. A large oil painting of his Majesty the Czar of Russia hangs over the marble chimneypiece.

It is growing dark. Already a wintry wilderness of garden without, upon which snow and sleet are pitilessly beating, is barely discernible. By the window looms, through the dusk, the shadowy shape of an enormous stuffed tiger, crouched as if about to spring upon a spare white-haired man in neat dark green uniform, who, seated at a writing-table covered with papers and official documents, has just settled himself more comfortably in a roomy armchair. With a pleasant smile, and a long pull at a freshly lit "papirosh," he gives vent to his feelings with the remark that heads this chapter.

There is silence for a while, unbroken save by the crackle of blazing logs and occasional rattle of driving sleet against the window-panes. It is the 5th of January (O.S.). I am at Tiflis, in the palace of Prince Dondoukoff Korsákoff, Governor of the Caucasus, and at the present moment in that august personage's presence.

"Ceci non!" repeats the prince a second time, in answer to my request; adding impatiently, "They should know better in London than to send you to me. The War Minister in St. Petersburg alone has power to grant foreigners permission to visit Central Asia. You must apply to him, but let me first warn you that it is a long

[1] The sacred image of the Saviour or Holy Virgin.

business. No"—after a pause—"no; were I in your place I would go to Persia. It is a country replete with interest."

I know, from bitter experience of Russian officials, that further parley is useless. Making my bow with as good a grace as possible under the circumstances, I take leave of the governor and am escorted by an aide-de-camp, resplendent in white and gold, through innumerable vestibules, and down the great marble staircase, to where my sleigh awaits me in the cutting north-easter and whirling snow. Gliding swiftly homewards along the now brilliantly lit boulevards, I realize for the first time that mine has been but a wild-goose chase after all; that, if India is to be reached by land, it is not *viâ* Merv and Cábul, but by way of Persia and Baluchistán.

The original scheme was a bold one, and I derive some consolation in the thought that the journey would most probably have ended in defeat. This was the idea. From Tiflis to Baku, and across the Caspian to Ouzoun Áda, the western terminus of the Trans-Caspian Railway. Thence by rail to Merv and Bokhára, and from the latter city direct to India, *viâ* Balkh and Cábul, Afghanistán. A more interesting journey can scarcely be conceived, but Fate and the Russian Government decreed that it was not to be. Not only was I forbidden to use the railway, but (notwithstanding the highest recommendation from the Russian Ambassador in London) even to set foot in Trans-Caspia.

The old adage, "delay is dangerous," is never so true as when applied to travel. The evening of my interview with the governor, I had resolved, ere retiring to rest, to make for India *viâ* Teherán. My route beyond that city was, perforce, left to chance, and the information I hoped to gain in the Shah's capital.

Tiflis, capital of the Caucasus, is about midway between the Black and Caspian seas, and lies in a valley between two ranges of low but precipitous hills. The river Kúr, a narrow but swift and picturesque stream spanned by three bridges, bisects the city, which is divided in three parts: the Russian town, European colony, and Asiatic quarter. The population of over a hundred thousand is indeed a mixed one. Although Georgians form its bulk, Persia contributes nearly a quarter, the rest being composed of Russians, Germans, French, Armenians, Greeks, Tartars, Circassians, Jews, Turks, and Heaven knows what besides.[2]

Tiflis is a city of contrasts. The principal boulevard, with its handsome stone buildings and shops, tramways, gay cafés, and electric light, would compare favourably with the Nevski Prospect in St. Petersburg, or almost any first-class European thoroughfare; and yet, almost within a stone's throw, is the Asiatic quarter, where the traveller is apparently as far removed from Western civilization as in the most remote part of Persia or Turkestán. The Armenian and Persian bazaars are perhaps the most interesting. I doubt whether the streets of Yèzd or Bokhára present so strange and picturesque a sight, such vivid effects of movement and colour. Every race, every nationality, is represented, from the stalwart, ruddy-faced Russian soldier in flat white cap and olive-green tunic, to the grave, stately Arab merchant with huge turban and white draperies, fresh from Bagdad or Bussorah.

[2] The name Tiflis is derived from *Tbilis Kalaki*, or "Hot Town," so called from the hot mineral springs near which it stands.

Georgians and Circassians in scarlet tunics and silver cartridge-belts, Turks in fez and frock-coat, Greeks and Albanians in snowy petticoats and black gaiters, Khivans in furs and quaint conical lamb's-wool hats, Tartars from the Steppes, Turkomans from Merv, Parsees from Bombay, African negroes,—all may be seen in the Tiflis Bazaar during the busy part of the day.

But woe to the luckless European who, tempted by the beauty of their wares, has dealings with the wily Persian merchant. There is a proverb in Tiflis that "It takes two Jews to rob an Armenian, two Armenians to rob a Persian," and the "accursed Faringi" is mercilessly swindled whenever he ventures upon a bargain.

With the exception of the aforesaid boulevard, the European quarter of Tiflis presents the same mixture of squalor and grandeur found in most Russian towns, St. Petersburg not excepted. There is the same dead, drab look about the streets and houses, the same absence of colour, the same indescribable smell of mud, leather, and drainage, familiar to all who have visited Asiatic Russia. I had intended remaining a couple of days, at most, in Tiflis, but my stay was now indefinitely prolonged. Such a severe winter had not been known for years. The mountain passes into Persia were reported impassable, and the line to Baku had for some days been blocked with snow.

My Russian Christmas (which falls, O.S., on our 6th of January) was not a cheerful one. A prisoner in a stuffy bedroom of the Hôtel de Londres, I sat at the window most of the day, consuming innumerable glasses of tea and cigarettes, watching the steadily falling snow, and wondering whether the weather would ever clear and allow me to escape from a place so full of unpleasant associations, and which had brought me so much disappointment and vexation. The loud laughter and bursts of song that ascended every now and then from the crowded *salle-á-manger* (for the Hôtel de Londres is the "Maison Dorée" of Tiflis) only served to increase my depression and melancholy. Had there been a train available, I verily believe I should have taken a ticket then and there, and returned to England!

But morning brings consolation in the shape of blue sky and dazzling sunshine. The snow has ceased, apparently for good. Descending to breakfast full of plans for the future, I find awaiting me an individual destined to play an important part in these pages—one Gerôme Realini, a Levantine Russian subject, well acquainted with the Persian language—who offers to accompany me to India as interpreter. His terms are moderate, and credentials first-rate. The latter include one from Baker Pasha, with whom he served on the Turkoman frontier expedition. More for the sake of a companion than anything else, I close with Gerôme, who, though he does not understand one word of English, speaks French fluently.

There is a very natural prejudice against the Levantine race, but my new acquaintance formed an exception to the rule. I never had reason to regret my bargain; a better servant, pluckier traveller, or cheerier companion no man could wish for. Gerôme had just returned from a visit to Bokhára, and his accounts of Central Asia were certainly not inviting. The Trans-Caspian railway was so badly laid that trains frequently ran off the line. There was no arrangement for water, travellers being frequently delayed three or four hours, while blocks of ice were melted for the boiler; while the so-called first-class carriages were filthy, and crowded with vermin. The advance of Holy Russia had apparently not improved Merv, which had become, since its annexation, a kind of inferior Port Said, a refuge for the scum, male and female, of St. Petersburg, Moscow, and Odessa. Drunkenness and debauchery reigned paramount. Low gambling-houses, *café chantants*, and less reputable establishments flourished under the liberal patronage of the Russian officers, who, out of sheer *ennui*, ruined their pockets and constitutions with drunken orgies, night and day. There was no order of any kind, no organized police-force, and robberies and assassinations took place almost nightly. Small-pox was raging in the place when Gerôme left it; also a loathsome disease called the "Bouton d'alep"—a painful boil which, oddly enough, always makes its appearance upon the body in odd numbers, never in even. It is caused by drinking or washing in unboiled water. Though seldom fatal, there is no cure for the complaint but complete change of climate.

We now set about making preparations for the journey. Provisions, saddlery, both had to be thought of; and, having laid in a small stock of Liebig, tea, biscuits, chocolate, and cigarettes (for space was limited), I proceeded, under Gerôme's guidance, to purchase a saddle. Seventy-five roubles bought a capital one, including bridle. Here let me advise those visiting Persia to follow my example, and buy their saddlery in Tiflis. There is a heavy duty payable on foreign saddles in Russia, and they are not one whit better, or indeed so well suited to the purpose, as those made in the Caucasus.

One hears a deal, in Europe, of the beauty of the Circassian and Georgian women. Although I remained in Tiflis over a week, I did not see a single pretty woman among the natives. As in every Russian town, however, the "Moushtaïd," or "Bois de Boulogne" of Tiflis, was daily, the theatre nightly, crowded with pretty faces of the dark-eyed, oval-faced Russian type. The new opera-house, a handsome building near the governor's palace, is not yet completed.

The Hôtel de Londres was the favourite *rendezvous* after the play. Here till the small hours assembled nightly the *élite* of European Tiflis. Russian and Georgian officers in gorgeous uniforms of dark green, gold lace, and astrachan; French and German merchants with their wives and daughters; with a sprinkling of *demi-mondaines* from Odessa or Kharkoff, sipping tea or drinking kummel and "kakèti" at the little marble tables, and discussing the latest scandals. Kakèti, a wine not unlike Carlowitz, is grown in considerable quantities in the Caucasus. There are two kinds, red and white, but the former is considered the best. Though sound and good, it is cheap enough—one rouble the quart. Tobacco is also grown in small quantities in parts of Georgia and made into cigarettes, which are sold in Tiflis at three kopeks per hundred. But it is poor, rank stuff, and only smoked by the peasantry and droshki-drivers.

TIFLIS

Tiflis has a large and important garrison, but is not fortified. Its topographical depôt is one of the best in Russia, and I managed, not without some difficulty, to obtain from it maps of Afghanistán and Baluchistán. The latter I subsequently found better and far more accurate than any obtainable in England. The most insignificant hamlets and unimportant camel-tracks and wells were set down with extraordinary precision, especially those in the districts around Kelát.

There is plenty of sport to be had round Tiflis. The shooting is free excepting over certain tracts of country leased by the Tiflis shooting-club. Partridge, snipe, and woodcock abound, and there are plenty of deer and wild boar within easy distance of the capital. Ibex is also found in the higher mountain ranges. For this (if for no other reason) Tiflis seems to be increasing in popularity every year for European tourists. It is now an easy journey of little over a week from England, with the advantage that one may travel by land the whole way from Calais. This route is *viâ* Berlin, Cracow, Kharkoff, and Vladikavkas, and from the latter place by coach (through the Dariel Gorge) to Tiflis.

The purchase of a warm astrachan bonnet, a bourka,[3] and bashlik,[4] completed my outfit. It now consisted of two small portmanteaus (to be changed at Teherán for saddle-bags), a common canvas sack for sleeping purposes, and a brace of revolvers. Gerôme was similarly accoutred, with the exception of the portmanteaus. My interpreter was evidently not luxuriously inclined, for his *impedimenta* were all contained in a small black leather hand-bag! All being ready, eleven o'clock on the night of the 12th of January found us standing on the platform of the Tiflis railway station, awaiting the arrival of the Baku train, which had been delayed by a violent storm down the line.

I received a letter from the governor a few hours before my departure, wishing me *bon voyage*, and enclosing a document to ensure help and civility from the officials throughout his dominions. It may seem ungrateful, but I felt that I could well have dispensed with this, especially as I was leaving his Excellency's government at Baku, a distance of only ten hours by rail.

It was again snowing hard, and the east wind cut through my bourka as if it had been a thin linen jacket. Seeking shelter in the crowded, stuffy waiting-room, we solaced ourselves with cigarettes and vodka till past 2 a.m., when the train arrived. Another delay of two hours now occurred, the engine having broken down; but the carriages, like those of most Russian railways, were beautifully warmed, and we slept soundly, undisturbed by the howling of the wind and shouting of railway officials. When I awoke, we were swiftly rattling through the dreary monotonous steppe country that separates Tiflis from the Caspian Sea.

The Russians may, according to English ideas, be uncivilized in many ways, but they are undoubtedly far ahead of other European nations, with the exception perhaps of France, as regards railway travelling. Although the speed is slow, nothing is left undone, on the most isolated lines, to ensure comfort, not to say luxury. Even in this remote district the refreshment-rooms were far above the average in England. At Akstafá, for instance, a station surrounded by a howling wilderness

[3] *Bourka,* a long sleeveless coat made of goatskin.

[4] *Bashlik,* the soft camel-hair hood and neckerchief in one, worn by Russian soldiers.

of steppe and marsh; well-cooked viands, game, pastry, and other delicacies, gladdened the eye, instead of the fly-blown buns and petrified sandwiches only too familiar to the English railway traveller. The best railway buffet I have ever seen is at Tiumen, the terminus of the Oural railway, and actually in Siberia.

Railway travelling has, however, one drawback in this part of Russia, which, though it does not upset the arrangements of a casual traveller, must seriously inconvenience the natives—the distance of stations from towns. We drank tea, a couple of hours or so before arriving at Baku, at a station situated more than one hundred versts[5] from the town of its name. The inhabitants of the latter seldom availed themselves of the railway, but found it easier, except in very bad weather, to drive or ride to the Caspian port.

The dull wintry day wears slowly away, as we crawl along past league upon league of wild steppe land. The *coup d'oeil* from our carriage-window is not inspiriting. It rests upon a bare, bleak landscape, rolling away to the horizon, of waves of drab and dirty-green land, unbroken save for here and there a pool of stagnant water, rotting in a fringe of sedge and rush, or an occasional flock of wild-fowl. At rare intervals we pass, close to the line, a Tartar encampment. Half a dozen dirty brown tents surrounded by horses, camels, and thin shivering cattle, the latter covered with coarse sack-clothing tied round their bellies to protect them from the cutting blast that sweeps from the coast across this land of desolation. None of the human population are visible, and no wonder. It must be cold enough outside. Even in this well-warmed compartment one can barely keep feet and fingers from getting numbed.

It is almost dark when, towards six o'clock, there appears, far ahead, a thin streak of silver, separating the dreary brown landscape from the cold grey sky.

"We have nearly arrived, monsieur," says Gerôme. "There is the Caspian Sea."

[5] A *verst* is about three-quarters of a mile.

CHAPTER II.

THE CASPIAN—ASTARÁ—RÉSHT.

I arrived in Baku on (the Russian) New Year's Eve, and found railway officials, porters, and droshki-drivers all more or less fuddled with drink in consequence. With some difficulty we persuaded one of the latter to drive us to the hotel, a clean and well-appointed house, a stone's throw from the quay. Our Isvostchik[6] was very drunk. His horses, luckily for us, were quiet; for he fell off his box on the way, and smilingly, but firmly, declined to remount. Gerôme then piloted the troika safely to our destination, leaving Jehu prone in the mud.

Baku, a clean, well laid-out city of sixty thousand inhabitants, is the most important town on the shores of the Caspian. Its name is said to be derived from the Persian words *bad,* "the wind," and *kubeda,* "beaten," signifying "Wind-beaten;" and this seems credible, for violent storms are prevalent along the coast. The town is essentially European in character. One can scarcely realize that only fifty years ago a tumble-down Persian settlement stood on the spot now occupied by broad, well-paved, gas-lit streets, handsome stone buildings, warehouses, and shops. Baku has, like Tiflis, a mixed population. Although Russians and Tartars form its bulk, France, Germany, Italy, Greece, Turkey, and Persia are all represented, most of the Europeans being employed in the manufacture of petroleum. The naphtha springs are said to yield over 170,000 tons of oil yearly.

A French engineer, Mr. B——, whose acquaintance I made at the hotel, described Baku as terribly monotonous and depressing to live in after a time. There is not a tree or sign of vegetation for miles round the town—nothing but bleak, desolate steppe and marsh, unproductive of sport and cultivation, or, indeed, of anything save miasma and fever. In summer the heat, dust, and flies are intolerable; in winter the sun is seldom seen. There is no amusement of any kind—no *café,* no band, no theatre, to go to after the day's work. This seemed to distress the poor Parisian exile more than anything, more even than the smell of oil, which, from the moment you enter until you leave Baku, there is no getting away from. Although the wells are fully three miles away, the table-cloths and napkins were saturated with it, and the very food one ate had a faint sickly flavour of naphtha. "I bathed in the Caspian once last summer," said Mr. B———, despairingly, "and did not get the smell out of my skin for a week, during which time my friends forbade me their houses! Mon Dieu! Quel pays!"

The steamer for Enzelli was to leave at eleven. Having wished my French

---

[6] *Isvostchik,* a cab-driver.

friend farewell, and a speedy return to his native country, we set out for the quay. The night was fine, but away to our left dense clouds of thick black smoke obscured the lights of the town and starlit sky, while the furnaces of the "Tchornigorod"[7] blazed out of the darkness, their flames reflected in the dark waters of the Caspian, turning the little harbour into a lake of fire.

The landing stage is crowded with passengers—a motley crowd of Russian officials, soldiers, peasants, and Tartars. With difficulty we struggle through the noisy, drunken rabble, for the most part engaged in singing, cursing, fighting, and embracing by turns, and succeed at last in finding our ship, the *Kaspia*, a small steamer of about a hundred and fifty tons burthen. The captain is, fortunately for us, sober, which is more than can be said of the crew. Alongside us lies the *Bariatinsky*, a large paddle-steamer bound for Ouzounada, the terminus of the Trans-Caspian Railway. She also is on the point of departure, and I notice, with relief, that most of the crowd are making their way on board her.

The passenger-steamers on the Caspian are the property of the Caucase-Mercure Company, a Russian firm. They are, with few exceptions, as unseaworthy as they are comfortless, which says a great deal. All are of iron, and were built in England and Sweden, sent to St. Petersburg by sea, there taken to pieces and despatched overland to Nijni-Novgorod, on the Volga. At Nijni they were repieced and taken down the Volga to the Caspian.

The *Bariatinsky* was first away, her decks crammed with soldiers bound for Central Asia. They treated us to a vocal concert as the ship left port, and I paced the moonlit deck for some time, listening to the sweet sad airs sung with the pathos and harmony that seems born in every Russian, high or low. I retired to rest with the "Matoushka Volga," a boat-song popular the length and breadth of Russia, ringing in my ears.

There are no private cabins on board the *Kaspia*. I share the stuffy saloon with a greasy German Jew (who insists on shutting all the portholes), an Armenian gentleman, his wife, and two squalling children, a Persian merchant, and Gerôme.

The captain's cabin, a box-like retreat about eight feet square, leads out of our sleeping-place, which is also used as a drawing and dining-room. As the latter it is hardly desirable, for the German and Persian are both suffering violently from *mal-de-mer* before we have been two hours out, and no wonder. Though there is hardly a perceptible swell on, the tiny cock-boat rolls like a log. To make matters worse, the *Kaspia's* engines are worked by petroleum, and the smell pursues one everywhere.

The passage from Baku to Enzelli (the port of Résht) is usually made in a little over two days in *fine weather*. All depends upon the latter, for no vessel can enter if it is blowing hard. There is a dangerous bar with a depth of barely five feet of water across the mouth of the harbour, and several Europeans, impatient of waiting, have been drowned when attempting to land in small boats. "I frequently have to take my passengers back to Baku," said Captain Z—— at the meal he was pleased

[7] "Tchornigorod," or "Black Town," so called from the smoke that hangs night and day over the oil-factories.

to call breakfast; "but I think we shall have fine weather to-morrow." I devoutly hoped so.

Little did I know what was in store for us; for the glass at midday was falling-fast, and at 2 p.m., when we anchored off Lenkorán, it was snowing hard and blowing half a gale.

The western coasts of the Caspian are flat and monotonous. There are two ports of call between Baku and Enzelli—Lenkorán, a dismal-looking fishing-village of mud huts, backed by stunted poplars and a range of low hills; and Astará, the Russo-Persian frontier. Trade did not seem very brisk at either port. We neither landed nor took in cargo at either. A few small boats came out to the ship with fish to sell. The latter is bad and tasteless in the Caspian, with the exception of the sturgeon, which abounds during certain seasons of the year. The fisheries are nearly all leased by Russians, who extract and export the caviar. There is good shooting in the forests around Lenkorán, and tigers are occasionally met with. The large one in the possession of Prince Dondoukoff Korsákoff, mentioned in the first chapter, was shot within a few miles of the place.

We arrived off Astará about 6.30 that evening. It was too dark to see anything of the place, but I had, unfortunately for myself, plenty of opportunities of examining it minutely a couple of days later. We weighed anchor again at nine o'clock, hoping, all being well, to reach Enzelli at daybreak. The sea had now gone down, and things looked more promising.

My spirits rose at the thought of being able to land on the morrow. I was even able to do justice to the abominable food set before us at dinner—greasy sausages and a leathery beefsteak, served on dirty plates and a ragged table-cloth that looked as if it had been used to clean the boiler. But the German Jew had recovered from his temporary indisposition, the cadaverous Persian had disappeared on deck, and the Armenian children had squalled themselves to sleep, so there was something, at least, to be thankful for. Captain Z——, a tall, fair-haired Swede, who spoke English fluently, had been on this line for many years, and told us that for dangerous navigation, violent squalls, and thick fogs the Caspian has no equal. Many vessels are lost yearly and never heard of again. He also told us of a submarine city some miles out of Baku, called by the natives "Tchortorgorod," or "City of the Devil." "In calm, sunny weather," said Z——, "one can distinctly make out the streets and houses." The German Jew, of a facetious disposition, asked him whether he had not also seen people walking about; but Z—— treated the question with contemptuous silence.

Man is doomed to disappointment. I woke at daylight next morning; to find the *Kaspia* at anchor, pitching, rolling, and tugging at her moorings as if at any moment the cable might part. Every now and again a sea would crash upon the deck, and the wind, howling through the rigging, sounded like the yelling of a thousand fiends. Hurrying on deck, I learn the worst. A terrific sea is running, and the glass falling every hour. One could scarcely discern, through the driving mist, the long low shore and white line of breakers that marked the entrance to Enzelli. To land was out of the question. No boat would live in such a sea. "I will lay-to till this evening," said Captain Z— —. "If it does not then abate, I fear you must make up your mind to return to Baku, and try again another day." A pleasant prospect indeed!

A DIRTY NIGHT IN THE CASPIAN

I have seldom passed a more miserable twenty-four hours. The weather got worse as the day wore on. Towards midday it commenced snowing; but this, instead of diminishing the violence of the gale, seemed only to increase it. Even the captain's cheery, ruddy face clouded over, as he owned that he did not like the look of things. "Had I another anchor, I should not mind," he said; calmly adding, "If this one parts, we are lost!" I thought, at the time, he might have kept this piece of information to himself. Meanwhile nothing was visible from the cabin-windows but great rollers topped with crests of foam, which looked as if, every moment, they would engulf the little vessel. But she behaved splendidly. Although green seas were coming in over the bows, flooding her decks from stem to stern, and pouring down the gangway into the saloon, the *Kaspia* rode through the gale like a duck. To venture on deck was impossible. One could barely sit, much less stand, and the atmosphere of the saloon may be better imagined than described. Every aperture tightly closed; every one, with the exception of the captain, Gerôme, and myself, sea-sick; no food, no fire, though we certainly did not miss the former much.

About ten o'clock Z— — weighed anchor and stood out to sea. It would not be safe, he said, to trust to our slender cable another night. About midnight I struggled on deck, to get a breath of fresh air before turning in. The night was fine and clear, but the sea around black as ink, with great foaming white rollers. The decks, a foot deep in snow, were deserted save by Z— — and the steersman, whose silhouettes stood out black and distinct against the starlit sky as they paced the rickety-looking little bridge flanked by red and green lights. The Enzelli lighthouse was no longer visible. The latter is under the care of Persians, who light it, or not, as the humour takes them. This is, on dark nights, a source of considerable danger to shipping; but, though frequently remonstrated with by the Russian Government, the Shah does not trouble his head about the matter.

Three routes to Teherán were now open to us: back to Baku, thence to Tiflis, and over the mountains to Talriz,—very dubious on account of the snow; the second, from Baku to Astrabad, and thence *viâ* Mount Demavend,—still more dubious on account of bad landing as well as blocked passes; there remained to us Astará, and along the sea-beach (no road) to Enzelli, with swollen rivers and no post-horses. All things considered, we resolved to land at Astará, even at the risk of a ducking. Daylight found us there, anchored a mile from the shore, and a heavy swell running. But there is no bar here; only a shelving sandy beach, on which, even in rough weather, there is little danger. Some good-sized boats came out to the *Kaspia* with fish and vegetables, and we at once resolved to land. Anything sooner than return to Baku!

"There is no road from Astará," said Z— —, "and deep rivers to cross. You will be robbed and murdered like the Italian who travelled this way three years ago! He was the last European to do so."

Gerôme remembers the incident. In fact, he says, the murdered man was a friend of his, travelling to Teherán with a large sum of money. Unable to land at Résht, and impatient to reach his destination, he took the unfrequented route, was waylaid, robbed, tied to a tree, and left to starve. "He was alone and unarmed, though," says my companion; adding with a wink, "Let them try it on with us!"

Seeing remonstrance is useless, Z— — wishes us God-speed. The good-natured Swede presses a box of Russian cigarettes into my hand as I descend the ladder—a gift he can ill afford—and twenty minutes later our boat glides safely and smoothly on Persian soil.

It was a lovely day, and the blue sky and sunshine, singing of birds, and green of plain and forest, a pleasant relief to the eye and senses after the cold and misery of the past two days. Astará (though the port of Tabriz) is an insignificant place, its sole importance lying in the fact that it is a frontier town. On one side of the narrow river a collection of ramshackle mud huts, neglected gardens, foul smells, beggars, and dogs—Persia; on the other, a score of neat stone houses, well-kept roads and paths, flower-gardens, orchards, a pretty church, and white fort surrounded by the inevitable black-and-white sentry-boxes, guarded by a company of white-capped Cossacks—Russia. I could not help realizing, on landing at Astará, the huge area of this vast empire. How many thousand miles now separated me from the last border town of the Great White Czar that I visited—Kiakhta, on the Russo-Chinese frontier?

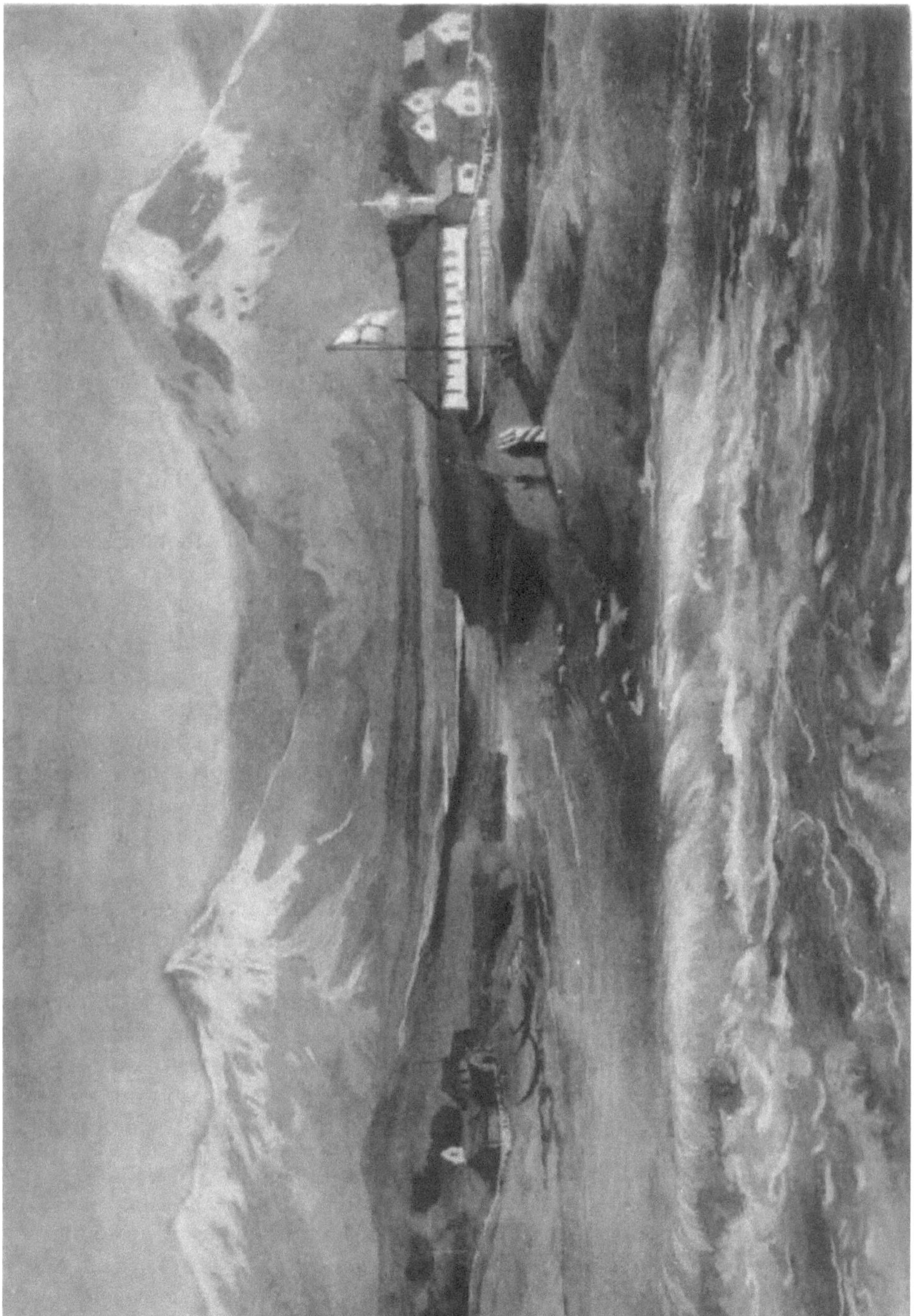

ASTARÁ, RUSSO-PERSIAN FRONTIER

Surrounded by a ragged mob, we walked to the village to see about horses and a lodging for the night. The latter was soon found—a flat-roofed mud hut about thirty feet square, devoid of chimney or furniture of any kind. The floor, cracked in several places, was crawling with vermin, and the walls undermined with rat-holes; but in Persia one must not be particular. Leaving our baggage in the care of one "Hassan," a bright-eyed, intelligent-looking lad, and instructing him to prepare a meal, we made for the bazaar, a hundred yards away, through a morass, knee deep in mud and abomination of all kinds, to procure food.

A row of thirty or forty mud huts composed the "bazaar," where, having succeeded in purchasing tea, bread, eggs, and caviar, we turned our attention to horseflesh.

An old Jew having previously agreed to convert, at exorbitant interest, our rouble notes into "sheis" and keráns, negotiations for horses were then opened by Gerôme, and, as the *patois* spoken in Astará is a mixture of Turkish and Persian, with a little Tartar thrown in, his task was no easy one, especially as every one spoke at once and at the top of their voices. We discovered at last that but few of the villagers owned a horse, and those who did were very unwilling to let the animal for such an uncertain journey. "Who is going to guarantee that the 'Farangis' will not steal it?" asked one ragged, wild-looking fellow in sheepskins and a huge lamb's-wool cap. "Or get it stolen from them?" added another, with a grin. "They can have my old grey mare for two hundred keráns, but you won't catch me letting her for hire," added a third.

With the aid of our friend, the Jew, however, we finally persuaded the sheepskin gentleman (a native of Khiva) to change his mind. After considerable haggling as to price, he disappeared, to return with two of the sorriest steeds I ever set eyes on. "We ought to reach Enzelli in about three days, if we do not get our throats cut," said the Khivan, who was to accompany us, encouragingly.

Hassan had been busy in our absence; he had prepared an excellent pilaff, and sent to Russian Astará for some kakèti wine, which was brought over in a goatskin. This, with our own provisions bought in the morning, furnished a substantial and much-needed meal. Persian native bread is somewhat trying at first to a weak digestion. It is unleavened, baked in long thin strips, and is of suet-like consistency. The hut, like most native houses in Persia, had no chimney, the only outlet for the smoke being through the narrow doorway. This necessitates lying flat on one's back in the clear narrow space between smoke and flooring, or being suffocated—a minor inconvenience as compared with others in Persian travel.

The Khivan arrived with the horses at six next morning. By seven o'clock we were well on the road, which for the first ten miles or so led by the sea-shore, through dense thickets of brushwood, alternating with patches of loose drifting sand. I was agreeably disappointed in the ponies; for though it was deep, heavy going, they stepped out well and freely. The clear sunshine, keen air, and lovely scenery seemed to have the same inspiriting effect on them as on ourselves.

The *coup d'œil* was indeed a lovely one. To our right a glorious panorama of palm, forest, and river stretched away for miles, bounded on the horizon by a chain of lofty precipitous mountains, their snowy peaks white and dazzling against the deep cloudless blue, their grassy slopes and rocky ravines hidden, here and there, by grey mists floating lazily over depths of dark green forest at their feet. To our left broad yellow sands, streaked with seaweed and dark driftwood, and cold grey waters of the Caspian Sea—colourless and dead even under this Mediterranean sky, and bringing one back, so to speak, from a beautiful dream to stern reality.

About midday we came to a broad but fordable river, which the Khivan called the Chulàmak. We all crossed in safety, notwithstanding the deep holes our guide warned us against, and which, as the water was thick and muddy, gave Gerôme and myself some anxiety. The stream was about fifty yards across and much swollen by the snow. Landing on the other side ahead of my companions, I rode on alone, and presently found myself floundering about girth-deep in a quicksand. It was only with great difficulty that we extricated the pony. These quicksands are common on the shores of the Caspian, and natives, when travelling alone, have perished from this cause.

Nothing occurred worthy of notice till about 3 p.m., when we reached the river Djemnil. An arm of the sea more accurately describes this stream, which is (or was at the time of which I write) over three hundred yards across. Here we had some difficulty with the Khivan, who was for encamping till morning. I, however, strongly objected to sleeping *a la belle étoile*, especially as the sky had now clouded over, and it was beginning to snow. Partly by conciliation, partly by threats, we at last persuaded him to make the attempt, following closely in his wake. It was nasty work. Twice our horses were carried off their feet by the strong current running out to sea (we were only a quarter of a mile from the mouth); and once we, or rather the horses, had to swim for it; but we reached the opposite shore in under half an hour, wet and numbed to the waist, but safe. At seven we were snugly housed for the night at Katvesera, a so-called village of three or four mud hovels, selecting the best (outwardly) for our night's lodging. We were badly received by the natives. Neither money nor threats would induce them to produce provisions of any kind, so we fell back on sticks of chocolate and Valentine's meat-juice. The latter I never travel without—it is invaluable in uncivilized and desert countries.

The inhabitants of Katvesera are under a score in number, and live chiefly on fish, though I noticed in the morning that a considerable quantity of land was under cultivation—apparently rice and barley. They were a sullen, sulky lot, and we had almost to take the hut by force. The Khivan, Gerôme, and myself took it in turns to watch through the night. It was near here that the Italian was assassinated.

A start was made at daybreak. The weather had now changed. A cutting north-easter was blowing, accompanied with snow and sleet. We forded, about 11 a.m., the Kokajeri river, a mountain stream about thirty yards wide, unfordable except upon the sea-beach. At midday we halted at Tchergári, a fishing-village on the shores of the Caspian.

Tchergári contains about two hundred inhabitants, mostly fishermen employed by a Russian firm. The houses, built of tree-trunks plastered with mud, had roofs of thatched reed, and were far more substantial and better built than any I had yet seen in Persia. Fearing a reception like that of the previous evening, we had intended riding straight through the place to our destination for the night, when a European advanced to meet us through the snow. Mr. V— —, a Russian, and overseer of the fishery, had made his hut as comfortable as circumstances would admit, and we were soon seated before a blazing fire (with a chimney!), discussing a plate of steaming shtchi,[8] washed down by a bottle of kakèti. Roast mutton and pastry followed, succeeded by coffee and vodka (for we had the good luck to arrive at our host's dinner-hour). By the time cigarettes were under way we felt fully equal to the long cold ride of fifteen miles that separated us from our night's halting-place, Alalá. Résht itself seemed at least thirty miles nearer than it had before dinner.

"You are bold," said Mr. V— —, in French, "to attempt this journey at this time of year. I do not mean as regards footpads and robbers; reports concerning them are always greatly exaggerated; but the rivers are in a terrible state. There is one just beyond Alalá, that I know you cannot cross on horseback. I will send a man on at once to try and get a boat for you, and you can pull the horses after you. There is an Armenian at Alalá, who will give you a lodging to-night" Mr. V— —'s good fare and several glasses of vodka considerably shortened our ride, and we arrived at Alalá before dark, where a hearty welcome awaited us. Turning in after a pipe and two or three glasses of tea, we slept soundly till time to start in the morning. The outlook from our snug resting-place was not inviting—the sky of a dirty grey, blowing hard, and snowing harder than ever.

Alalá contains about eight hundred inhabitants. The land surrounding it is thickly cultivated with rice and tobacco. Neither are, however, exported in any quantity, the difficulties of transport to Astará or Enzelli being so great.

It is somewhat puzzling to a stranger to get at the names of places on the southern shores of the Caspian. Most of the villages are known by more than one, but Alalá rejoices in as many *aliases* as an old gaol-bird, viz. Alalá, Asalim, and Navarim.

Thanks to our Russian friend, a boat and a couple of men were awaiting us at the big river (I could not ascertain its name). Entering it ourselves, we swam the horses over one by one. It took us the best part of two hours. Though only two hundred yards wide, they were off their legs nearly the whole way. What we should have done without Mr. V— —'s aid I know not.

Towards sundown the high tower of the Shah's palace at Enzelli came in sight. At last the neck of this weary journey was broken, and to-morrow, all being well, we should be at Résht. The road is winding, and it was not till past ten o'clock that we rode through the silent, deserted streets to the caravanserai, a filthier lodging than any we had yet occupied. But, though devoured by vermin, I slept soundly, tired out with cold and fatigue. We dismissed the Khivan with a substantial *pourboire*. He had certainly behaved extremely well for one of his race.

Enzelli is an uninteresting place. It has but two objects of interest (in Persian eyes)—the lighthouse (occasionally lit) and a palace of the Shah, built a few years

[8] Russian cabbage-soup.

since as a *pied-à-terre* for his Majesty on the occasion of his visits to Europe. It is a tawdry gimcrack edifice, painted bright blue, red, and green, in the worst possible taste. The Shah, on returning from Europe last time, is said to have remarked to his ministers on landing at Enzelli, "I have not seen a single building in all Europe to compare with this!" Probably not—from one point of view.

The Caspian may indeed be called a Russian lake, for although the whole of its southern coast is Persian, the only Persian vessel tolerated upon it by Russia is the yacht of the Shah, a small steamer, the gift of the Caucase-Mercure Company, which lies off Enzelli. Even this vessel is only permitted to navigate in and about the waters of the Mourdab ("dead water"), a large lake, a kind of encroachment of the sea, eighteen to twenty miles broad, which separates Enzelli from Peri-Bazar, the landing-place for Résht, four miles distant. The imperial yacht did once get as far as Astará (presumably by mistake), but was immediately escorted back to Enzelli by a Russian cruiser. There is, however, a so-called Persian fleet—the steamship *Persepolis*, anchored off Bushire, in the Persian Gulf, and the *Susa*, which lies off Mohammerah. The former is about six hundred tons, and carries four Krupp guns; but the latter is little better than a steam-launch. Both have been at anchor for about four years, and are practically unseaworthy and useless.

We embarked at nine o'clock, in a boat pulled by eight men. The crossing of the Mourdab is at times impossible, owing to the heavy sea; but this time luck was with us, and midday saw us at Peri-Bazar, where there is no difficulty in procuring riding-horses to take one into Résht. The country between the two places was formerly morass and jungle, but on the occasion of the Shah's visit to Europe about twenty years ago, a carriage-road was made—not a good one, for such a thing does not exist in Persia—but a very fair riding-track (in dry weather). We reached Résht wet to the skin, the snow having ceased and given way to a steady downpour of rain.

Résht bears the unpleasant reputation of being the most unhealthy city in Persia. Its very name, say the natives, is derived from the word *rishta*, "death." "If you wish to die," says a proverb of Irak, "go to Résht!" The city, which had, at the beginning of the century, a population of over sixty thousand inhabitants, now has barely thirty thousand. This certainly looks as if there were some truth in the foregoing remarks; and there is no doubt that, on the visitation of the plague about ten years ago, the mortality was something frightful. A great percentage of deaths are ascribed to Résht fever—a terrible disease, due to the water and the exhalations from the marshes surrounding the city. It is certainly the dampest place in the world. The sun is seldom seen, and one's clothes, even on a dry, rainless day, become saturated with moisture.

The town is, nevertheless, prettily situated in a well-wooded country. It would almost be imposing were it not for the heavy rains and dews, which cause a rapid decay of the buildings. The latter are mostly of red brick and glazed tiles.

Résht is the depôt for goods to and from Persia—chiefly silks. Tobacco is also grown in yearly increasing quantities. Several Russian firms have opened here for the manufacture of cigarettes, which, though they may find favour among the natives, are too hot and coarse for European tastes. They are well made and cheap enough—sevenpence a hundred.

In addition to the native population, Résht contains about five hundred Armenians, and a score or so of Europeans. Among the latter are a Russian and a British vice-consul. To the residence of the latter we repaired. Colonel Stewart's kindness and hospitality are a byword in Persia, and the Sunday of our arrival at Résht was truly a day of rest after the discomfort and privations we had undergone since leaving Baku.

CHAPTER III.

RÉSHT—PATCHINAR.

Day broke gloomily enough the morning following the day of our arrival at Résht. The snow, still falling fast, lay over two feet deep in the garden beneath my window, while great white drifts barred the entrance-gates of the Consulate. About eight o'clock our host made his appearance, and, waking me from pleasant dreams of sunnier climes, tried to dissuade me from making a start under such unfavourable circumstances. An imperial courier had just arrived from Teherán, and his report was anything but reassuring. The roads were in a terrible state; the Kharzán, a long and difficult pass, was blocked with snow, and the villages on either side of it crowded with weather-bound caravans.

The prospect, viewed from a warm and comfortable bed, was not inviting. Anxiety, however, to reach Teherán and definitely map out my route to India overcame everything, even the temptation to defer a journey fraught with cold, hunger, and privation, and take it easy for a few days, with plenty of food and drink, to say nothing of cigars, books, and newspapers, in the snug cosy rooms of the Consulate. "You will be sorry for it to-morrow," said the colonel, as he left the room to give the necessary orders for our departure; adding with a smile, "I suppose a wilful man must have his way."

There are two modes of travelling in Persia: marching with a caravan, a slow and tedious process; and riding post, or "chapar." The latter, being the quickest, is usually adopted by Europeans, but can only be done on the Government post-roads, of which there are five: from Teherán to Résht, Tabriz, Meshéd, Kermán, and the Persian Gulf port, Bushire. These so-called roads are, however, often mere caravan-tracks, sometimes totally hidden by drifting sand or snow. In the interior of the country the hard sun-baked soil is usually trackless, so that the aid of a "Shagird Chapar," or post-boy, becomes essential.

The distance between the "Chapar khanehs," as the tumble-down sheds doing duty for post-houses are called, is generally five farsakhs, or about twenty English miles; but the Persian farsakh is elastic, and we often rode more, at other times less, than we paid for. Travel is cheap: one kerán per farsakh (2½*d.* a mile) per horse, with a *pour-boire* of a couple of keráns to the "Shagird" at the end of the stage.

Given a good horse and fine weather, Persian travel would be delightful; but the former is, unfortunately, very rarely met with. Most of the post-horses have been sold for some vice which nothing but constant hard work will keep under. Kickers, rearers, jibbers, shyers, and stumblers are but too common, and falls of almost daily occurrence on a long journey. Goodness knows how many Gerôme and I had between Résht and the Persian Gulf.

Notwithstanding these drawbacks, the speed attained by the wretched half-starved animals is little short of marvellous. Nothing seems to tire them. We averaged fifty miles a day after leaving Teherán, covering, on one occasion, over a hundred miles in a little over eleven hours. This is good work, considering the ponies seldom exceed fourteen hands two inches, and have to carry a couple of heavy saddle-bags in addition to their rider. Gerôme must have ridden quite fourteen stone.

About ten o'clock the horses arrived, in charge of a miserable-looking Shagird, in rags and a huge lamb's-wool cap, the only warm thing about him. It was pitiful to see the poor wretch, with bare legs and feet, shivering and shaking in the cutting wind and snow. The ponies, too, looked tucked up and leg-weary, as if they had just come off a long stage (which, indeed, they probably had) instead of going on one.

"Don't be alarmed; they are the proverbial rum 'uns to look at," said our host, who would not hear of our setting out without saddle-bags crammed with good things: cold meat, sardines, cigarettes, a couple of bottles of brandy, and a flask of Russian vodka. But for these we must literally have starved *en route*.

"Good-bye. Good luck to you!" from the colonel.

"En avant!" cries Gerôme, with a deafening crack of his heavy chapar whip. We are both provided with this instrument of torture—a thick plaited thong about five feet long, attached to a short thick wooden handle, and terminating in a flat leathern cracker of eight or ten inches. A cut from this would make an English horse jump out of his skin, but had little or no effect on the tough hides of our "chapar" ponies. The snow is almost up to the knees of the latter as we labour through the gateway and into the narrow street. Where will it be on the Kharzán Pass?

Résht is picturesquely situated. It must be a lovely place in summer-time, when fertile plains of maize, barley, and tobacco stretch away on every side, bounded by belts of dark green forest and chains of low well-wooded hills, while the post-road leads for miles through groves of mulberry trees, apple orchards, and garden-girt villas, half hidden by roses and jasmine. But this was hardly a day for admiring the beauties of nature. Once out of the suburbs and in the open country, nothing met the eye but a dreary wilderness of white earth and sullen grey sky, that boded ill for the future. The cold was intense. Although dressed in the thickest of tweeds and sheepskin jacket, sable pelisse, enormous "bourka," and high felt boots, it was all I could do to keep warm even when going at a hand gallop, varied every hundred yards or so by a desperate "peck" on the part of my pony.

The first stage, Koudoum, five farsakhs from Résht, was reached about three o'clock in the afternoon. This was my first experience of a Chapar khaneh. The Shagird informed us that it was considered a very good one, and was much frequented by Europeans in summer-time—presumably, judging from the holes in the roof, for the sake of coolness. Let me here give the reader a brief description of the accommodation provided for travellers by his Imperial Majesty the Shah. The Koudoum Chapar khaneh is a very fair example of the average Persian post-house.

Imagine a small one-storied building, whitewashed, save where wind and rain have disclosed the brown mud beneath. A wooden ladder (with half the rungs missing) leads to the guest-chamber, a large bare room, devoid of furniture of any kind, with smoke-blackened walls and rotten, insecure flooring. A number of rats scamper away at our approach. I wonder what on earth they can find to eat, until Gerôme points out a large hole in the centre of the apartment. This affords an excellent view of the stables, ten or twelve feet below, admitting, at the same time, a pungent and overpowering odour of manure and ammonia. A smaller room, a kind of ante-chamber, leads out of this. As it is partly roofless, I seek, but in vain, for a door to shut out the icy cold blast. Further search in the guest-room reveals six large windows, or rather holes, for there are no shutters, much less window-panes. It is colder here, if anything, than outside, for the draughts are all ways at once; but we must in Persia be thankful for small mercies. There is a chimney, in which a good log fire, kindled by Gerôme, is soon blazing.

Lunch and a nip of the colonel's vodka work wonders, and we are beginning to think, over a "papirosh," that Persia is not such a bad place after all, when the Shagird's head appears at the window. There are only two horses available for the next stage, but a third has been sent for from a neighbouring village, and will shortly arrive. As night is falling fast, I set out with the Shagird for the next station, Rustemabad, leaving Gerôme, who has already travelled the road and knows it well, to follow alone.

It is still snowing fast, but my mount is a great improvement on that of the morning, luckily, for the stage is a long one, and we have a stiff mountain to climb before reaching our destination for the night.

We ride for three hours, slowly and silently, over a plain knee-deep in snow. About half-way across a tinkle of bells is heard, clear and musical, in the distance. Presently a large caravan looms out of the dusk—fifty or sixty camels and half a dozen men. The latter exchange a cheery "Good night" with my guide. Slowly the ungainly, heavily laden beasts file past us, gaunt and spectral in the twilight, the bells die away on the still wintry air, and we are again alone on the desolate plain—not a sign of life, not a sound to be heard, but the crunching of snow under our horses' feet, and the occasional pistol-like crack of my guide's heavy whip.

It is almost dark when we commence the ascent of the mountain on the far side of which lies Rustemabad. The path is rough and narrow, and in places hewn out of the solid rock. Towards the summit, where a slip or false step would be fatal, a dark shapeless mass appears, completely barring the pathway, on the white snow. Closer inspection reveals a dead camel, abandoned, doubtless, by the caravan we have just passed, for the carcase is yet warm. With considerable difficulty, but aided by the hard slippery ground, we drag it to the brink of the precipice, and send it crashing down through bush and briar, to fall with a loud splash into a foaming torrent far below. During this performance one of the ponies gets loose, and half an hour is lost in catching him again.

So the journey wore on. Half-way down on the other side of the mountain, my pony stumbled and shot me head first into a pool of liquid mud, from which I was, with some difficulty, extricated wet through and chilled to the bone. The discomfort was bad enough, but, worse still, my sable pelisse, the valuable gift of a Russian friend, was, I feared, utterly ruined.

It was nearly nine o'clock when we reached Rustemabad, to find rather worse quarters than we had left at Koudoum. To make matters worse, I had no change of clothes, and the black, ill-smelling mud had penetrated to the innermost recesses of my saddle-bags, which did not tend to improve the flavour of the biscuits and chocolate that constituted my evening meal. No food of any kind was procurable at the post-house, and all our own provisions were behind with Gerôme. Luckily, I had stuck to the flask of vodka!

With the help of the postmaster, a decrepit, half-witted old man, and the sole inmate of the place, I managed to kindle a good fire, and set to work to dry my clothes, a somewhat uncomfortable process, as it entailed my remaining three-parts naked for half the night in an atmosphere very little above zero. The sables were in a terrible state. It was midnight before the mud on them was sufficiently dry to brush off, as I fondly hoped, in the morning.

Gerôme did not turn up till one o'clock a.m., his horse not having arrived at Koudoum till past seven. He had lost his way twice, and had almost given up all hopes of reaching Rustemabad till daylight, when my fire, the only light in the place, shone out of the darkness. The poor fellow was so stiff and numbed with fatigue and cold that I had to lift him off his horse and carry him into the post-house. He was a sorry object, but I could not refrain from smiling. My companion's usually comical, ruddy face wore a woebegone look, while long icicles hung from his hair, eyebrows, and moustaches, giving him the appearance of a very melancholy old Father Christmas.

Morning brought a cloudless blue sky and brilliant sunshine. My first thought on awaking was for the pelisse. Summoning the old postmaster, I confided the precious garment to him, with strict injunctions to take it outside, beat it well with a stick, and bring it back to me to brush. In the mean time, we busied ourselves with breakfast and a cup of steaming cocoa, for a long ride was before us. It was still bitterly cold, with a strong north-easter blowing. The thermometer marked (in the sun) only one degree above zero.

Rustemabad, a collection of straggling, tumble-down hovels, contains about four or five hundred inhabitants. The post-house, perched on the summit of a steep hill, is situated some little distance from the village, which stands in the centre of a plateau, bounded on the south-west by a chain of precipitous mountains. The country around is fertile and productive, being well watered by the Sefid Roud (White River). Rice is largely grown, but to-day not a trace of vegetation is visible; nothing but the vast white plain, smooth and unbroken, save where, here and there, a brown village blurrs its smooth surface, an oasis of mud huts in this desert of dazzling snow.

An exclamation from Gerôme suddenly drew my attention to the postmaster, who stood at the open doorway, my pelisse in hand. I was then unused to the ways and customs of the Persian peasantry, or should have known that it was but labour lost to make one spring at the old idiot, and, twining my fingers in his throat, shake him till he yelled for mercy. Nothing but a thick stick has the slightest effect upon the Shah's subjects; and I was, for a moment, sorely tempted to use mine. The reader must own that I should have been justified. It was surely enough to try the patience of a saint, for the old imbecile had deliberately walked down to the river, made a hole in the ice, and soaked the garment in water to the waist, reducing it to its former condition of liquid slime. This was *his* method of getting the mud off. I may add that this intelligent official had *assisted me in the drying process up till midnight.*

There was no help for it; nothing to be done but cut off the damaged portion from the waist to the heels—no easy matter, for it was frozen as stiff as a board. "It will make a better riding-jacket now," said Gerôme, consolingly; "but this son of a pig shall not gain by it," he added, stamping the ruined remains into the now expiring fire.

The village of Patchinar, at the foot of the dreaded Kharzán Pass, was to be our halting-place for the night. The post-road, after leaving Rustemabad, leads through the valley of the Sefid Roud river, in which, by the way, there is excellent salmon-fishing. About six miles from Rustemabad is a spot called by the natives the "Castle of the Winds," on account of the high winds that, even in the calmest weather, prevail there. Although, out on the plain, there was a scarcely perceptible breeze, we had to literally fight our way against the terrific gusts that swept through this narrow gorge. Fortunately, it was a fine day, but the fine powdery snow whirled up and cut into our eyes and faces, and made travelling very unpleasant.

These violent wind-storms have never been satisfactorily accounted for. They continue for a certain number of hours every day, summer and winter, increasing in force till sunset, when they abate, to rise again the following dawn. On some occasions horses, and even camels, have been blown over, and caravans are sometimes compelled to halt until the fury of the storm has diminished.

Crossing a ridge of low hills, we descended into the valley of Roudbar, a quiet and peaceful contrast to the one we had just left. The wind now ceased as if by magic. Much of the snow had here disappeared under the warm sunshine, while before us, nestling in a grove of olive trees, lay the pretty village, with its white picturesque houses and narrow streets shaded by gaily striped awnings. It was like a transformation-scene, this sudden change from winter, with its grey sky and cold icy blast, to the sunny stillness and repose of an English summer's day. We rode through the bazaar, a busy and crowded one for so small a place. A large trade is done here in olives. Most of it is in the hands of two enterprising Frenchmen, who started business some years ago, and are doing well.

We managed to get a mouthful of food at Menjil while the horses were being changed.

Colonel S—— had especially warned us against sleeping here, the Chapar khaneh being infested with the Meana bug, a species of camel tick, which inflicts a poisonous and sometimes dangerous wound. It is only found in certain districts, and rarely met with south of Teherán. The virus has been known, in some cases, to bring on typhoid fever, and one European is said to have died from its effects. For the truth of this I cannot vouch; but there is no doubt that the bite is always followed by three or four days' more or less serious indisposition.

CHAPTER IV.

PATCHINAR—TEHERÁN.

Our troubles commenced in real earnest at Patchinar, a desolate-looking place and filthy post-house, which was reached at sunset. The post from Teherán had just arrived, in charge of a tall strapping fellow armed to the teeth, in dark blue uniform and astrachan cap, bearing the Imperial badge, the lion and sun, in brass. The mail was ten days late, and had met with terrible weather on the Kharzán. They had passed, only that morning, two men lying by the roadway, frozen to death. The poor fellows were on their way to Teherán from Menjil, and had lain where they fell for two or three days. "You had far better have remained at Résht," added our informant, unpleasantly recalling to my mind the colonel's prophecy, "You will be sorry for this to-morrow!"

Notwithstanding hunger and vermin, we managed to enjoy a tolerable night's rest. The post-house was warm at any rate, being windowless. Patchinar was evidently a favourite halting-place, for the dingy walls of the guest-room were covered with writing and pencil sketches, the work of travellers trying to kill time, from the Frenchman who warned one (in rhyme) to beware of the thieving propensities of the postmaster, to the more practical Englishman, who, in a bold hand, had scrawled across the wall, *"Big bugs here!"* I may add that my countryman was not exaggerating.

There was no difficulty in getting horses the next morning. The post, which left for Résht before we were stirring, had left us seven sorry-looking steeds, worn out with their previous day's journey through the deep snow-drifts of the Kharzán. By nine o'clock we were ready to start, notwithstanding the entreaties of the postmaster, whose anxiety, however, was not on our account, but on that of the horses.

"I don't believe I shall ever see them again!" he mumbled mournfully, as we rode out of the yard. "And who is to repay me for their loss? You will be dead, too, before sundown, if the snow catches you in the mountains!"

But there seemed no probability of such a contingency. The sky was blue and cloudless, the sun so bright that the glare off the snow soon became unbearable without smoked goggles. The promise of an extra kerán or two if we reached the end of the stage by daylight had a wonderful effect on the Shagird. Though it was terribly heavy going, and the snow in places up to our girths, we covered the five miles lying between Patchinar and the foot of the Kharzán in a little over three hours—good going considering the state of the road. We were as often off the former as on it, for there was nothing to guide one; nothing but telegraph poles and wires were visible, and these are occasionally laid straight across country away from the track.

Our destination for the night was the village of Kharzán, which is situated near the summit of the mountain, about six thousand feet high. The ascent is continuous and precipitous. An idea may be gained of the steepness by the fact that we now left the valley of the Shah Roud, barely one thousand feet above sea-level, to ascend, in a distance of about twelve miles, over six thousand feet.

The Kharzán Pass is at all times dreaded by travellers, native and European, even in summer, when there are no avalanches to fear, snow-drifts to bar the way, or ice to render the narrow, tortuous pathway even more insecure. A serious inconvenience, not to say danger, is the meeting of two camel caravans travelling in opposite directions on the narrow track, which, in many places, is barely ten feet broad, and barely sufficient to allow two horses to pass each other, to say nothing of heavily laden camels. But to-day we were safe so far as this was concerned. Not a soul was to be seen in the clefts and ravines around, or on the great white expanse stretched out beneath our feet, as we crept cautiously up the side of the mountain, our guide halting every ten or fifteen yards to probe the snow with a long pole and make sure that we had not got off the path.

A stiff and tedious climb of nearly seven hours brought us to within a mile of the summit. Halting for a short time, we refreshed ourselves with a couple of biscuits and a nip of brandy, and proceeded on our journey. We had now arrived at the most dangerous part of the pass. The pathway, hewn out of the solid rock, and about ten feet wide, was covered with a solid layer of ice eight or ten inches thick, over which our horses skated about in a most uncomfortable manner. There was no guard-rail or protection of any sort on the precipice side. All went well for a time, and I was beginning to congratulate myself on having reached the summit without accident, when Gerdme's horse, just in front of me, blundered and nearly lit on his head. "Ah, son of a pig's mother!" yelled the little Russian in true Cossack vernacular, as the poor old screw, thoroughly done up, made a desperate peck, ending in a slither that brought him to within a foot of the brink. "That was a close shave, monsieur!" he continued, as his pony struggled back into safety, "I shall get off and walk. Wet feet are better than a broken neck any day!"

The words were scarcely out of his mouth, when a loud cry from the Shagird, and a snort and struggle from the pack-horse behind, attracted my attention. This time the beast had slipped with a vengeance, and was half-way over the edge, making, with his fore feet, frantic efforts to regain *terra firma* while his hind legs and quarters dangled in mid-air. There was no time to dismount and render assistance. The whole thing was over in less than ten seconds. The Shagird might, indeed, have saved the fall had he kept his head instead of losing it. All he could do was, with a loud voice and outstretched arms, to invoke the assistance of "Allah!" We were not long in suspense. Slowly, inch by inch, the poor brute lost his hold of the slippery ground, and disappeared, with a shrill neigh of terror, from sight. For two or three seconds we heard him striking here and there against a jutting rock or shrub, till, with a final thud, he landed on a small plateau of deep snow-drifts at least three hundred feet below. Here he lay motionless and apparently dead, while we could see through our glasses a thin stream of crimson flow from under him, gradually staining the white snow around.

CROSSING THE KHARZÁN

A cat is popularly supposed to have nine lives. After my experience of the Persian post-horse, I shall never believe that that rough and ill-shaped but useful animal has less than a dozen. The fall I have described would assuredly have killed a horse of any other nationality, if I may use the word. It seemed, on the contrary, to have a tonic and exhilarating effect on this Patchinar pony. Before we could reach him (a work of considerable difficulty and some risk) he had risen to his feet, given himself a good shake, and was nibbling away at a bit of gorse that peeped through the snow on which he had fallen. A deep cut on the shoulder was his only injury, and, curiously enough, our portmanteaus, with the exception of a broken strap, were unharmed. There was, luckily, nothing breakable in either.

Kharzán, a miserable village under snow for six months of the year, was reached without further mishap. There is no post-house, and the caravanserai was crowded with caravans. Before sundown, however, we were comfortably installed in the house of the headman of the place, who spread carpets of soft texture and quaint design in our honour, regaled us with an excellent "pilaff," and produced a flask of Persian wine. The latter would hardly have passed muster in Europe. The cork consisted of a plug of cotton-wool plastered with clay; the contents were of a muddy-brown colour. "It is pure Hamadán," said our host with pride, as he placed the bottle before us. "Perhaps the sahib did not know that our country is famous for its wines." It was not altogether unpalatable, something like light but rather sweet hock; very different, however, in its effects to that innocent beverage, and one could not drink much with impunity. Its cheapness surprised me: one shilling a quart bottle. That, at least, is the price our host charged—probably more than half again its real value.

The winegrowers of Hamadán have many difficulties to contend with; among others, the severe cold. In winter the wine is kept in huge jars, containing six or seven hundred bottles. These are buried in the ground, their necks being surrounded by hot beds of fermenting horse-dung, to keep the wine from freezing. But even this plan sometimes fails, and it has to be chopped out in solid blocks and melted for drinking.

Kharzán has a population of about a thousand inhabitants. It was here that Baker Pasha was brought some years ago in a dying condition, after being caught in a wind-storm on the Kharzán Pass, and lay for three days in the house we were lodging at. Our old friend showed us a clasp-knife presented him by the colonel, who on that occasion nearly lost both his feet from frost-bite. Captains Gill and Clayton,[9] of the Royal Engineers and Ninth Lancers, were with him, but escaped unharmed.

Stiff and worn out with the events of the day, we soon stretched ourselves in front of the blazing fire in anticipation of a good night's rest; but sleep was not for us. In the next room were a party of Persian merchants from Astrakhan on their way to Bagdad *viâ* Teherán, who had been prisoners here for five days, and were now carousing on the strength of getting away on the morrow. A woman was with them—a brazen-faced, shrill-voiced Armenian, who made more noise

[9] Both have since met violent deaths. Captain Gill was murdered by natives with Professor Palmer near Suez, and Captain Clayton killed while playing polo in India.

than all the rest put together. Singing, dancing, quarrelling, and drinking went on without intermission till long past midnight, our neighbours raising such a din that the good people of Kharzán, a quarter of a mile away, must have turned uneasily in their slumbers, and wondered whether an army of fiends had not broken loose. Towards 1 a.m. the noise ceased, and we were just dropping to sleep, when, at about half-past two in the morning, our drunken friends, headed by the lady, burst into our apartment, with the information, in bad Russian, that a gang of fifty men sent that morning to clear a path through the deep snow had just returned, and the road to Mazreh was now practicable. The caravans would be starting in an hour, they added. "And you'd better travel with them," joined in the lady, contemptuously, "or you will be sure to get into trouble by yourselves." A reply more forcible than polite from Gerôme then cleared the apartment; and, rekindling the now expiring embers, we prepared for the road.

We set out at dawn for the gate of the village, where the caravans were to assemble. It was still freezing hard, and the narrow streets like sheets of solid ice, so that our horses kept their legs with difficulty. We must have numbered fifty or sixty camels, and as many mules and horses, all heavily laden.

Daybreak disclosed a weird, beautiful scene: a sea of snow, over which the rising sun threw countless effects of light and colour, from the cold slate grey immediately around us, gradually lightening to the faintest tints of rose and gold on the eastern horizon, where stars were paling in a cloudless sky. Portrayed on canvas, the picture would have looked unnatural, so brilliant were the hues thrown by the rising sun over the land-, or rather snow-scape. The cold, though intense, was not unbearable, for there was fortunately no wind, and the spirits rose with the crisp, bracing air, brilliant sunshine, and jangle of caravan bells, as one realized that Teherán was now well within reach, and the dreaded Kharzán a thing of the past. Gerôme gave vent to his feelings with a succession of roulades and operatic airs; for my little friend had a very good opinion of his vocal powers, which I, unfortunately, did not share. But he was a cheery, indefatigable creature, and of indomitable pluck, and one gladly forgave him this, his only failing.

It was terribly hard work all that morning, and Gerôme had four, I three, falls, on one occasion wrenching my right ankle badly. Some of the drifts through which we rode must have been at least ten or fifteen feet deep. Some tough faggots thrown over these afforded a footing, or we should never have got over. Towards midday Mazreh was sighted; and we pushed on ahead, leaving the caravan to its own devices. The going was now better, and it was soon far behind us, the only object visible from the low hills which we now ascended, the camels and mules looking, from this distance, like flies crawling over a huge white sheet.

Lunch at Mazreh consisted of damp, mouldy bread, and some sweet, sickly liquid the postmaster called tea. Procuring fresh horses without difficulty, we set out about 3 p.m. for Kazvin. It was not till 10 p.m. that we were riding through the great gate of that city, which the soldier on guard consented, with some demur, to open.

Kazvin boasts a hotel and a boulevard! The latter is lit by a dozen oil-lamps;

the former, though a palatial building of brick, with verandahs and good rooms, is left to darkness and the rats in the absence of travellers. Having groped our way for half an hour or so about a labyrinth of dark, narrow streets, we presently emerged on the dimly lit boulevard (three of the oil-lamps had gone out), and rode up to the melancholy looking hostelry at the end. Failing to obtain admission, we burst open the door, and made ourselves as comfortable as circumstances would allow. Food was out of the question; drink, saving some villainous raki of Gerôme's, also; but there was plenty of firewood, and we soon had a good fire in the grate. This hotel was originally built by the Shah for the convenience of himself and ministers when on his way to Europe. It is only on these rare occasions that the barn-like building is put in order. Visions of former luxury were still visible in our bedroom in the shape of a bedstead, toilet-table, and looking-glass. "But we can't eat *them*!" said Gerôme, mournfully.

Kazvin, which now has a population of 30,000, has seen better days. It was once capital of Persia, with 120,000 inhabitants. Strolling out in the morning before breakfast, I found it well and regularly built, and surrounded by a mud wall, with several gates of beautiful mosaic, now much chipped and defaced.

Being the junction of the roads from Tabriz on the west, and Résht on the north to the capital, is now Kazvin's sole importance. The road to Teherán was made some years ago at enormous expense by the Shah; but it has now, in true Persian style, been left to fall into decay. It is only in the finest and driest weather that the journey can be made on wheels, and this was naturally out of the question for us. A railway was mooted some time since along this, the only respectable carriage-road in Persia—but the project was soon abandoned.

The post-houses, however, are a great improvement on any in other parts of the country. At Kishlak, for instance, we found a substantial brick building with a large guest-room, down the centre of which ran a long table with spotless table-cloth, spread out with plates of biscuits, apples, nuts, pears, dried fruits, and sweetmeats, beautifully decorated with gold and silver paper, and at intervals decanters of water—rather cold fare with the thermometer at a few degrees above zero. The fruits and biscuits were shrivelled and tasteless, having evidently been there some months. It reminded me of a children's doll dinner-party. With the exception of these Barmecide feasts and some straw-flavoured eggs, there was nothing substantial to be got in any of the post-houses till we reached our destination.

About four o'clock on the 27th we first sighted the white peak of Mount Demavend, and by three o'clock next day were within sight of the dingy brown walls, mud houses, and white minarets of the city of the Shah—Teherán.

CHAPTER V.

TEHERÁN.

A brilliant ball-room, pretty faces, smart gowns, good music, and an excellent supper;—thus surrounded, I pass my first evening in Teherán, a pleasant contrast indeed to the preceding night of dirt, cold, and hunger.

But it was not without serious misgivings that I accepted the courteous invitation of the German Embassy. The crossing of the Kharzán had not improved the appearance of dress-clothes and shirts, to say nothing of my eyes being in the condition described by pugilists as "bunged up," my face of the hue of a boiled lobster, the effects of sun and snow.

One is struck, on entering Teherán, with the apparent cleanliness of the place as compared with other Oriental towns. The absence of heaps of refuse, cess-pools, open drains, and bad smells is remarkable to one accustomed to Eastern cities; but this was perhaps, at the time of my visit, due to the pure rarified atmosphere, the keen frosty air, of winter. Teherán in January, with its cold bracing climate, and Teherán in June, with the thermometer above ninety in the shade, are two very different things; and the town is so unhealthy in summer, that all Europeans who can afford to do so live on the hills around the capital.

The environs are not picturesque. They have been likened to those of Madrid, having the same brown calcined soil, the same absence of trees and vegetation. The city, viewed from outside the walls, is ugly and insignificant, and, on a dull day, indistinguishable at no great distance. In clear weather, however, the beehive-like dwellings and rumbling ramparts stand out in bold relief against a background of blue sky and dazzling snow-mountains, over which towers, in solitary grandeur, the peak of Mount Demavend,[10] an extinct volcano, over 20,000 feet high, the summit of which is reported by natives to be haunted. The ascent is gradual and easy, and has frequently been made by Europeans.

Teherán is divided into two parts—the old city and the new. In the former, inhabited only by natives, the streets are narrow, dark, and tortuous, leading at intervals into large squares with deep tanks of running water in the centre. The latter are characteristic of Persia, and have in summer a deliciously cool appearance, the coping of the fountain being only an inch or so in height, and the water almost flush with the ground. The new, or European quarter, is bisected by a broad tree-lined thoroughfare, aptly named the "Boulevard des Ambassadeurs," for here

[10] The word *Demavend* signifies literally "abundance of mist," so called from the summit of this mountain being continually wreathed in clouds.

are the legations of England, France, and Germany. The Russian Embassy, a poor building in comparison with the others, stands in another part of the town. Hard by the English Embassy is the Hôtel Prevôt, kept by a Frenchman of that name, once confectioner-in-chief to his Majesty the Shah. Here we took up our quarters during our stay in the capital.

At the extremity of the Boulevard des Ambassadeurs is the "Place des Canons," so called from the old and useless cannon of various ages that surround it. The square is formed by low barn-like barracks, their whitewashed walls decorated with gaudy and rudely drawn pictures of Persian soldiers and horses. Beyond this again, and approached by an avenue of poplar trees, lit by electric light, is the palace of the Shah, with nothing to indicate the presence in town of the sovereign but a guard of ragged-looking, unkempt Persians in Russian uniform lounging about the principal gateway.

The Persian soldier is not a credit to his country. Although drilled and commanded by European officers, he is a slouching, awkward fellow, badly paid, ill fed, and not renowned for bravery. The ordinary infantry uniform consists of a dark-blue tunic and trousers with red facings, and a high astrachan busby with the brass badge of the lion and sun. To a stranger, however, the varied and grotesque costumes in which these clowns are put by their imperial master is somewhat confusing. One may see, for instance, Russian cossacks, French chasseurs, German uhlans, and Austrian cuirassiers incongruously mixed up together in the ranks on parade. His army is the Shah's favourite toy, and nothing affords the eccentric monarch so much amusement as constant change of uniform. As the latter are manufactured in and sent out from the countries they represent, the expense to the state is considerable.

The first Europeans to instruct this rabble were Frenchmen, but England, Russia, Germany, and Austria have all supplied officers and instructors within the past fifty years, without, however, any good result. Although the arsenal at Teherán is full of the latest improvements in guns and magazine rifles, these are kept locked up, and only for show, the old Brown Bess alone being used. The Cossack regiment always stationed at Teherán, ostensibly for the protection of the Shah, and officered by Russians, is the only one with any attempt at discipline or order, and is armed with the Berdán rifle.

The Teherán bazaar is, at first sight, commonplace and uninteresting. Though of enormous extent (it contains in the daytime over thirty thousand souls), it lacks the picturesque Oriental appearance of those of Cairo or Constantinople, where costly and beautiful wares are set out in tempting array before the eyes of the unwary stranger. Here they are kept in the background, and a European must remain in the place for a couple of months or so, and make friends with the merchants, before he be even permitted to see them. The position is reversed. At Stamboul the stranger is pestered and worried to buy; at Teherán one must sometimes entreat before being allowed even to inspect the contents of a silk or jewel stall. Even then, the owner will probably remain supremely indifferent as to whether the "Farangi" purchase or not. This fact is curious. It will probably disappear with the advance of civilization and Mr. Cook.

TEHERÁN

Debouching from the principal streets or alleys of the bazaar, which is of brick, are large covered caravanserais, or open spaces for the storage of goods, where the wholesale merchants have their warehouses. The architecture of some of these caravanserais is very fine. The cool, quiet halls, their domed roofs, embellished with delicate stone carving, and blue, white, and yellow tiles, dimly reflected in the inevitable marble tank of clear water below, are a pleasant retreat from the stifling alleys and sun-baked streets. Talking of tanks, there seems to be no lack of water in Teherán. I was surprised at this, for there are few countries so deficient in this essential commodity as Persia. It is, I found, artificially supplied by "connaughts," or subterranean aqueducts flowing from mountain streams, which are practically inexhaustible. In order to keep a straight line, shafts are dug every fifty yards or so, and the earth thrown out of the shaft forms a mound, which is not removed. Thus a Persian landscape, dotted with hundreds of these hillocks, often resembles a field full of huge ant-hills. The mouths of these shafts, left open and unprotected, are a source of great danger to travellers by night. Teherán is provided with thirty or forty of these aqueducts, which were constructed by the Government some years ago at enormous expense and labour.

As in most Eastern cities, each trade has its separate alley or thoroughfare in the Teherán bazaar. Thus of jewellers, silk mercers, tailors, gunsmiths, saddlers, coppersmiths, and the rest, each have their separate arcade. The shops or stalls are much alike in appearance, though they vary considerably in size. Behind a brick platform, about three feet wide and two feet in height, is the shop, a vaulted archway, in the middle of which, surrounded by his wares, kalyan[11] or cigarette in mouth, squats the shopkeeper. There are no windows. At night a few rough boards and a rough Russian padlock are the sole protection, saving a smaller apartment at the back of each stall, a kind of strong-room, guarded by massive iron-bound doors, in which the most valuable goods are kept. There is no attempt at decoration; a few only of the jewellers' shops are whitewashed inside, the best being hung with the cheapest and gaudiest of French or German coloured prints. The stalls are usually opened about 6.30 a.m., and closed at sunset. An hour later the bazaar is untenanted, save for the watchmen and pariah dogs. The latter are seen throughout the day, sleeping in holes and corners, many of them almost torn to pieces from nightly encounters, and kicked about, even by children, with impunity. It is only at night that the brutes become really dangerous, and when, in packs of from twenty to thirty, they have been known to attack and kill men. Occasionally the dogs of one quarter of the bazaar attack those of another, and desperate fights ensue, the killed and wounded being afterwards eaten by the victors. It is, therefore, unsafe to venture out in the streets of Teherán after dark without a lantern and good stout cudgel.

From 11 to 12 a.m. is perhaps the busiest part of the day in the bazaar. Then is one most struck with the varied and picturesque types of Oriental humanity, the continuously changing kaleidoscope of native races from Archangel to the Persian Gulf, the Baltic Sea to Afghanistán.

---

[11] A pipe similar to the Turkish "hubble-bubble," wherein the tobacco is inhaled through plain or rose water.

Nor are contrasts wanting. Here is Ivanoff from Odessa or Tiflis, in the white peaked cap and high boots dear to every Russian, haggling over the price of a carpet with Ali Mahomet of Bokhára; there Chung-Yang, who has drifted here from Pekin through Siberia, with a cargo of worthless tea, vainly endeavouring to palm it off on that grave-looking Parsee, who, unfortunately for the Celestial, is not quite such a fool as he looks. Such a hubbub never was heard. Every one is talking or shouting at the top of their voices, women screaming, beggars whining, fruit and water sellers jingling their cymbals, while from the coppersmiths' quarter hard by comes a deafening accompaniment in the shape of beaten metal. Occasionally a caravan of laden camels stalk gravely through the alleys, scattering the yelling crowd right and left, only to reassemble the moment it has passed, like water in the wake of a ship. Again it separates, and a sedan, preceded by a couple of gholams with long wands, is carried by, and one gets a momentary glimpse of a pair of dark eyes and henna-stained finger-tips, as a fair one from the "anderoon"[12] of some great man is carried to her jeweller's or perfumer's. The "yashmak" is getting very thin in these countries, and one can form a very fair estimate of the lady's features (singularly plain ones) as the sedan swings by. Towards midday business is suspended for a while, and the alleys of the bazaar empty as if by magic. For nearly a whole hour silence, unbroken save by the snarling of some pariah dog, the hiss of the samovar, and gurgle of the kalyan, falls over the place, till 2 p.m., when the noise recommences as suddenly as it ceased, and continues unbroken till sunset.

On the whole, the bazaar is disappointing. The stalls for the sale of Persian and Central Asian carpets, old brocades and tapestries, and other wares dear to the lover of Eastern art, are in the minority, and must be hunted out. Manchester goods, cheap calicoes and prints, German cutlery, and Birmingham ware are found readily enough, and form the stock of two-thirds of the shops in the carpet and silk-mercers' arcade.

It is by no means easy to find one's way about. No one understands a word of English, French, or German, and had it not been for my knowledge of Russian—which, by the way, is the one known European language among the lower orders—I should more than once have been hopelessly lost.

Europeans in Teherán lead a pleasant though somewhat monotonous life. Summer is, as I have said, intolerable, and all who can seek refuge in the hills, where there are two settlements, or villages, presented by the Shah to England and Russia. Winter is undoubtedly the pleasantest season. Scarcely an evening passes without a dance, private theatricals, or other festivity given by one or other of the Embassies, entertainments which his Imperial Majesty himself frequently graces with his presence.

There is probably no living sovereign of whom so little is really known in Europe as Nasr-oo-din, "Shah of Persia," "Asylum of the Universe," and "King of Kings," to quote three of his more modest titles. Although he has visited Europe twice, and been made much of in our own country, most English people know absolutely nothing of the Persian monarch's character or private life. That he ate *entrées* with his fingers at Buckingham Palace, expressed a desire to have the Lord

[12] Harem.

Chamberlain bowstrung, and conceived a violent and unholy passion for an amiable society lady somewhat inclined to *embonpoint*, we are most of us aware; but beyond this, the Shah's *vie intime* remains, to the majority of us at least, a sealed book. This is perhaps a pity, for, like many others, Nasr-oo-din is not so black as he is painted, and, notwithstanding all reports to the contrary, is said, by those who should know, to be one of the kindest-hearted creatures breathing.

The government of Persia is that of an absolute monarchy. The Shah alone has power of life and death, and, even in the most remote districts, the assent of the sovereign is necessary before an execution can take place. The Shah appoints his own ministers. These are the "Sadr-Azam," or Prime Minister; the "Sapar-Sala," Commander-in-chief; "Mustof-al-Mamalak," Secretary of State, and Minister of Foreign Affairs. These are supposed to represent the Privy Council, but they very seldom meet, the Shah preferring to manage affairs independently. The total revenue of the latter has been estimated at seven million pounds sterling.

Nasr-oo-din, who is now sixty-five years of age, ascended the throne in 1848. His reign commenced inauspiciously with a determined attempt to assassinate him, made by a gang of fanatics of the Babi sect. The plot, though nearly successful, was frustrated, and the conspirators executed; but it is said that the Shah has lived in constant dread of assassination ever since. He is hypochondriacal, and, though in very fair health, is constantly on the *qui vive* for some imaginary ailment. The post of Court physician, filled for many years past by Dr. Tholozan, a Frenchman, is no sinecure.

The habits of the Shah are simple. He is, unlike most Persians of high class, abstemious as regards both food and drink. Two meals a day, served at midday and 9 p.m., and those of the plainest diet, washed down by a glass or two of claret or other light wine, are all he allows himself. When on a hunting-excursion, his favourite occupation, the Shah is even more abstemious, going sometimes a whole day without food of any kind. He is a crack shot, and is out nearly daily, when the weather permits, shooting over his splendid preserves around Teherán. There is no lack of sport. Tiger and bear abound; also partridge, woodcock, snipe, and many kinds of water-fowl; but the Shah is better with the rifle than the fowling-piece. The Shah is passionately fond of music, and has two or three string and brass bands trained and conducted by a Frenchman. When away on a long sporting-excursion, he is invariably accompanied by one of these bands.

Were it not for the running attendants in scarlet and gold, and the crimson-dyed[13] tail of his horse, no one would take the slim, swarthy old gentleman in black frock-coat, riding slowly through the streets, and beaming benignly through a huge pair of spectacles, for the great Shah-in-Shah himself. Yet he is stern and pitiless enough when necessary, as many of the Court officials can vouch for. But few have escaped the bastinado at one time or another; but in Persia this is not considered an indignity, even by the highest in the land. The stick is painful, certainly, but not a disgrace in this strange country.

Nasr-oo-din has three legal wives, and an unlimited number of concu-

[13] A badge of royalty in Persia.

bines. Of the former, the head wife, Shuku-Es-Sultana, is his own cousin and the great-granddaughter of the celebrated Fatti-Ali-Shah, whose family was so large that, at the time of his death, one hundred and twenty of his descendants were still living. Shuku-Es-Sultana is the mother of the "Valliad," or Crown Prince, now Governor of Tabriz. The second wife is a granddaughter of Fatti-Ali-Shah; and the third (the Shah's favourite) is one Anys-u-Dowlet. The latter is the best looking of the three, and certainly possesses the greatest influence in state affairs. Of the concubines, the mother of the "Zil-i-Sultan" ("Shadow of the King") ranks the first in seniority. The Zil-i-Sultan is, though illegitimate, the Shah's eldest son, and is, with the exception of his father, the most influential man in Persia, the heir-apparent (Valliad) being a weak, foolish individual, easily led, and addicted to drink and the lowest forms of sensuality.

With the exception of eunuchs, no male person over the age of ten is permitted in the seraglio, or anderoon, which is constantly receiving fresh importations from the provinces. Persians deny that there are any European women, but this is doubtful. The harems of Constantinople and Cairo are recruited from Paris and Vienna; why not those of Teherán? The indoor costume of the Persian lady must be somewhat trying at first to those accustomed to European toilettes. The skirt, reaching only to the knee, is full and *bouffé,* like an opera-dancer's, the feet and legs generally bare. The only becoming part of the whole costume is the tightly fitting zouave jacket of light blue or scarlet satin, thickly braided with gold, and the gauze head-dress embroidered with the same material, and fastened under the chin with a large turquoise, ruby, or other precious stone.

Some of the women (even among the concubines) are highly educated; can play on the "tar",[14] or harmonica, sing, and read and write poetry; but their recreations are necessarily somewhat limited. Picnics, music, story-telling, kalyan and cigarette smoking, sweetmeat-making, and the bath, together with somewhat less innocent pastimes, form the sum total of a Persian concubine's amusements. Outside the walls of the anderoon they are closely watched and guarded, for Persians are jealous of their women, and, even in the most formal social gatherings, there is a strict separation of the sexes. Its imperial master occasionally joins in the outdoor amusements of his harem; indeed, he himself invented a game a few years since, which sounds more original than amusing. A slide of smooth alabaster about twenty feet long, on an inclined plane, was constructed in one of his bath-houses. Down this the Shah would gravely slide into the water, followed by his seraglio. The sight must have been a strange one, the costumes on these occasions being, to say the least of it, scanty!

The Shah's greatest failing is, perhaps, vacillation. He is constantly changing his mind, on trifling matters chiefly, for his northern neighbours take care that he is more consistent in affairs of state. Two or three times, between his visits to Europe in 1871 and 1889, he has started with great pomp and a large retinue for the land of the "Farangi," but, on arrival at Résht, has returned to Teherán, without a word of warning to his ministers, or apparent reason for his sudden change of plans. These "false starts" became a recognized thing after a time, and when, in

[14] A stringed instrument played in the same way as the European guitar.

1888, his Majesty embarked on his yacht and set sail for Baku, it came as a surprise, pleasant or otherwise, to his subjects at Teherán. The final undertaking of the journey may have been advised by his astrologers, for the Shah is intensely superstitious, and never travels without them. Nor will he, on any account, start on a journey on a Friday, or the thirteenth day of the month.

PERSIAN DANCING-GIRL

The palace of Teherán is, seen from the outside, a shapeless, ramshackle structure. The outside walls are whitewashed, and covered with gaudy red and blue pictures of men and horses, the former in modern military tunics and shakos, the latter painted a bright red. The figures, rudely drawn, remind one of a charity schoolboy's artistic efforts on a slate, but are somewhat out of place on the walls of a royal residence. The interior of the "Ark," as it is called, is a pleasant contrast to the outside, although even here, in the museum, which contains some of the finest gems and *objets d'art* in the world, the various objects are placed with singular disregard of order, not to say good taste. One sees, for instance, a tawdrily dressed mechanical doll from Paris standing next to a case containing the "Darai Nor," or "Sea of Light," a magnificent diamond obtained in India, and said to be the largest yet discovered, though somewhat inferior in quality to the "Koh-i-noor." A cheap and somewhat dilapidated cuckoo-clock and toy velocipede flank the famous globe of the world in diamonds and precious stones. This, the most costly and beautiful piece of workmanship in the place, is about eighteen inches in diameter, and is said to have cost eight millions of francs. The different countries are marked out with surprising accuracy and detail,—Persia being represented by turquoises, England by diamonds, Africa by rubies, and so on, the sea being of emeralds.

The museum itself is about sixty feet in length by twenty-five feet broad, its ceiling composed entirely of looking-glasses, its parquet flooring strewn with priceless Persian rugs and carpets. Large oil-paintings of Queen Victoria, the Czar of Russia, and other sovereigns, surround the walls, including two portraits of her Majesty the Ex-Empress Eugenie. It would weary the reader to wade through a description of the Jade work and *cloisonné*, the porcelain of all countries, the Japanese works of art in bronze and gold, and last, but not least, the cut and uncut diamonds and precious stones, temptingly laid out in open saucers, like *bonbons* in a confectioner's shop. The diamonds are perhaps the finest as regards quality, but there is a roughly cut ruby surmounting the imperial crown, said to be the largest in the world.

Though it was very cold, and the snow lay deep upon the ground, my stay at Teherán was not unpleasant. The keen bracing air, brilliant sunshine, and cloudless blue sky somewhat made amends for the sorry lodging and execrable fare provided by mine host at the Hôtel Prevôt. I have seldom, in my travels, come across a French inn where, be the materials ever so poor, the landlord is not able to turn out a decent meal. I have fared well and sumptuously at New Caledonia, Saigon, and even Pekin, under the auspices of a French innkeeper; but at Teherán (nearest of any to civilized Europe) was compelled to swallow food that would have disgraced a fifth-rate *gargotte* in the slums of Paris. Perhaps Monsieur Prevôt had become "Persianized"; perhaps the dulcet tones of Madame P., whose voice, incessantly rating her servants, reminded one of unoiled machinery, and commenced at sunrise only to be silenced (by exhaustion) at sunset, disturbed him at his culinary labours. The fact remains that the *cuisine* was, to any but a starving man, uneatable, the bedroom which madame was kind enough to assign to me, pitch dark and stuffy as a dog-kennel.

A long conference with General S——, an Austrian in the Persian service, decided my future movements. The general, one of the highest geographical authorities on Persia, strongly dissuaded my attempting to reach India *viâ* Meshéd and Afghanistán. "You will only be stopped and sent back," said he; "what is the use of losing time?" I resolved, therefore, after mature deliberation, to proceed direct to Ispahán, Shiráz, and Bushire, and from thence by steamer to Sonmiani, on the coast of Baluchistán. From the latter port I was to strike due north to Kelát and Quetta, and "that," added the general, "will bring you across eighty or a hundred miles of totally unexplored country. You will have had quite enough of it when you get to Kelát—if you ever *do* get there," he added encouragingly.

The route now finally decided upon, preparations were made for a start as soon as possible. Portmanteaus were exchanged for a pair of light leather saddle-bags, artistically embellished with squares of bright Persian carpet let in at the side, and purchased in the bazaar for twenty-two keráns, or about seventeen shillings English money. In these I was able to carry, with ease, a couple of tweed suits, half a dozen flannel shirts, three pairs of boots, and toilet necessaries, to say nothing of a box of cigars and a small medicine-chest. Gerôme also carried a pair of bags, containing, in addition to his modest wardrobe, our stores for the voyage—biscuits, Valentine's meat juice, sardines, tea, and a bottle of brandy; for, with the exception of eggs and Persian bread, one can reckon upon nothing eatable at the Chapar khanehs. There is an excellent European store shop at Teherán, and had it not been for limited space, we might have regaled on turtle soup, aspic jellies, quails, and *pâté de foie gras* galore throughout Persia. Mr. R. N——, an *attaché* to the British Legation at Teherán, is justly celebrated for his repasts *en voyage*, and assured me that he invariably sat down to a *recherché* dinner of soup, three courses, and iced champagne, even when journeying to such remote cities as Hamadán or Meshéd, thereby proving that, if you only take your time about it, you may travel comfortably almost anywhere—even in Persia.

CHAPTER VI.

TEHERÁN—ISPAHÁN.

We are already some farsakhs[15] from Teherán when day breaks on the 4th of February, 1889. The start is not a propitious one. Hardly have we cleared the Ispahán gate than down comes the Shagird's horse as if he were shot, breaking his girths and rider's thumb at the same moment. Luckily, we are provided with rope, and Persian saddles are not complicated. In ten minutes we are off again; but it is terribly hard going, and all one can do to keep the horses on their legs. Towards midday the sun slightly thaws the surface of the frozen snow, and makes matters still worse. Up till now the pace has not been exhilarating. Two or three miles an hour at most. It will take some time to reach India at this rate!

Four or five hours of this work, and there is no longer a sign of life to be seen on the white waste, saving, about a mile ahead of us, a thin wreath of grey smoke and half a dozen blackened tents—an encampment of gipsies. Far behind us the tallest minarets of the capital are dipping below the horizon, while to the left the white and glittering cone of Demavend stands boldly out from a background of deep cloudless blue. Though the sun is powerful—so much so, indeed, that face and hands are already swollen and blistered—the cold in the shade is intense. A keen, cutting north-easter sweeps across the white waste, and, riding for a time under the shadow of a low ridge of snow, I find my cigar frozen to my lips—nor can I remove it without painfully tearing the skin. Gerôme is in his element, and, as a natural consequence, my spirits fall as his rise. The slowness of our progress, and constant stumbling of my pony, do not improve the temper, and I am forced at last to beg my faithful follower to desist, for a time at least, from a vocal rendering of "La Mascotte" which has been going on unceasingly since we left Teherán. He obeys, but (unabashed) proceeds to carry on a long conversation with himself in the Tartar language, with which I am, perhaps happily, unacquainted. Truly he is a man of unfailing resource!

But even his angelic temper is tried when, shortly afterwards, we ride past the gipsy encampment. As he dismounts to light a cigarette out of the wind, one of the sirens in a tent catches sight of the little Russian, and in less than half a minute he is surrounded by a mob of dishevelled, half-naked females, who throw their arms about him, pull his hair and ears, and try, but in vain, to secure his horse and drag him into a tent. These gipsies are the terror of travellers in Persia, the men, most of them, gaining a precarious living as tinkers and leather-workers, with an occasional highway robbery to keep their hand in, the women living entirely by thieving

[15] A farsakh is about four miles.

and prostitution. The gentlemen of the tribe were, perhaps luckily for us, away from home on this occasion. One of the women, a good-looking, black-eyed girl, was the most persistent among this band of maenads, and, bolder than the rest, utterly refused to let Gerôme get on his pony, till, white with passion, the Russian raised his whip. This was a signal for a general howl of rage. "Strike me if you dare!" said the girl, her eyes ablaze. "If you do you will never reach the next station." But in the confusion Gerôme had vaulted into his saddle, and, setting spurs to our horses, we galloped or scrambled off as quick as the deep snow would allow us. "Crapule va!" shouted the little man, whose cheek and hair still bore traces of the struggle. "Il n'y a qu'en Perse qu'on fait des chameaus comme cela!"

Ispahán is about seventy farsakhs distant from Teherán. The journey has, under favourable conditions, been ridden in under two days, but this is very unusual, and has seldom been done except for a wager by Europeans. In our case speed was, of course, out of the question, with the road in the state it was. The ordinary pace is, on an average, six to eight miles an hour, unless the horses are very bad. It was nearly a week, however, before we rode through the gates of Ispahán, and even this was accounted a fair performance considering the difficulties we had to contend with.

Towards sunset the wind rose—a sharp north-easter that made face and ears feel as if they were being flogged with stinging-nettles. It was not until dusk that we reached Rabat Kerim, a small mud village, with a filthy windowless post-house. But a pigstye would have been welcome after such a ride, and the vermin which a flickering oil-lamp revealed in hundreds, on walls and flooring, did not prevent our sleeping soundly till morning. My thermometer marked only one degree above zero when we retired to rest, and the wood was too damp to light a fire. But we are in Persia!

It is only fair, however, to say that the road we were now travelling is not the regular post-road, which lies some distance to the eastward of Rabat Kerim, but was now impassable on account of the snow. The smaller track joins the main road at Koom. By taking the less frequented track, we were unable to go through the "Malak al Niote," or "Valley of the Angel of Death," which lies about half-way between the capital and Koom. The valley is so called from its desolate and sterile appearance, though, if this be so, the greater part of Persia might with reason bear the same name. Be this as it may, the Shagirds and natives have the greatest objection to passing through it after dark. A legend avers that it is haunted by monsters having the bodies of men and heads of beasts and birds. Surrounded by these apparitions, who lick his face and hands till he is unconscious, the traveller is carried away—where, history does not state—never to return.

If the first day's work had been hard, it was child's play compared to the second. The track, leading over a vast plain, had recently been traversed by a number of camel caravans, which had transformed it into a kind of Jacob's ladder formed by holes a couple of feet deep in the snow. As long as the horses trod into them all went well, but a few inches to the right or left generally brought them blundering on to their noses. The reader may imagine what a day of this work means. The strain on mind and muscle was almost unbearable, to say nothing of the blinding glare. Yet one could not but admire, during our brief pauses for rest, the picture before us. The boundless expanse of sapphire blue and dazzling white, with not a speck to mar it, save where, occasionally, the warm sun-rays had, here and there, laid bare chains of dark rocks, giving them the appearance of islands in this ocean of snow.

At Pitché, the midday station, no horses were to be had; so, notwithstanding that deep snow-drifts lay between us and Kushku Baïra, the halt for the night, we were compelled, after a couple of hours' rest, to set out on the ponies that had brought us from Rabat Kerim. More perhaps by good luck than anything else, we reached the latter towards 9 p.m. A bright starlit night favoured us, and, with the exception of a couple of falls apiece, we were none the worse. We found, too, to our great delight, a blazing fire burning in the post-house, kindled by some caravan-men. But there is always a saving clause in Persia. No water was to be had for love or money till the morning, and, knowing the raging thirst produced by melted snow, we had to forget our thirst till next day.

POST-HOUSE AT KUSHKU BAÏRA

A pleasant surprise also was in store for us. Two or three miles beyond Kushku Baïra we were clear of snow altogether. Not a vestige of white was visible upon the bare stony plain. Nothing but dull drab desert, stretching away on every side to a horizon of snow-capt hills, recalling, by their very whiteness, the miseries of the past two days. "Berik Allah!"[16] cried Gerôme. "We have done with the snow now." "Inshallah!"[17] I replied, though with an inward conviction that we should see it again further on, and suffer accordingly.

The sacred city of Koom[18] is one of the pleasantest recollections I retain of the ride between the capital and Ispahán. It was about two o'clock on the afternoon of the 6th of February that, breasting a chain of low sandy hills, the huge golden dome

[16] "Hurrah!"
[17] "Please God!"
[18] *Koom* signifies "sand."

of the Tomb of Fatima became visible. We were then still four miles off; but, even with our jaded steeds, the ride became what it had not yet been—a pleasure. The green sunlit plains of wheat and barley, interspersed with bars of white and red poppies, the picturesque, happy-looking peasantry, the strings of mule and camel caravans, with their gaudy trappings and clashing bells,—all this life, colour, and movement helped to give one new hope and energy, and drown the dreary remembrance of past troubles, bodily and mental. Even the caravans of corpses sent to Koom for interment, which we passed every now and again, failed to depress us, though at times the effluvia was somewhat overpowering, many of the bodies being brought to the sacred city from the most remote parts of Persia. Each mule bore two dead bodies, slung on either side, like saddle-bags, and one could clearly trace the outline of the figure wrapped in blue or grey cloth. A few of the friends and relatives of some of the deceased accompanied this weird procession, but the greater number of the dead had been consigned to the care of the muleteers. The latter, in true chalvadar[19] fashion, were stretched out flat on their stomachs fast asleep, their heads lolling over their animals, arms and legs dangling helplessly, while the caravan roamed about the track unchecked, banging their loads against each other, to the silent discomfiture of the unfortunate mourners.

A CORPSE CARAVAN

Koom is said to cover nearly twice as much ground as Shiráz, but more than half the city is in ruins, the Afghans having destroyed it in 1722. The principal buildings are mainly composed of mosques and sepulchres (for Koom is second only to Meshéd in sanctity), but most of them are in a state of decay and dilapidation. The mosque containing the Tomb of Fatima is the finest, its dome being covered with plates of silver-gilt—the natives say of pure gold. The sacred character

[19] Muleteer.

of this city is mainly derived from the fact that Fatima, surnamed "El Masouna" ("Free from sin"), died here many years ago. The tradition is that Fatima was on her way to the city of Tus, whither she was going to visit her brother, Imám Riza. On arrival at Koom, she heard of his death, which caused her to delay her journey and take up her residence here for a time, but she shortly afterwards sickened, and died of a broken heart. A mausoleum was originally built of a very humble nature, but, by order of Shah Abbas, it was enlarged and richly ornamented inside and out. Fatti-Ali-Shah and Abbas the Second are both buried here; also the wife of Mahomet Shah, who died in 1873, having had the dome of the mosque covered with gold. There is a legend among natives that Fatima's body no longer lies in the mosque, but was carried bodily to heaven shortly after death.

The population of Koom, which now amounts to little more than between ten and twelve thousand, was formerly much larger. Like many other Persian cities—saving, perhaps, Teherán—it retains but little of its greatness, either as regards art or commerce. The bazaar is, notwithstanding, extensive and well supplied. Koom is noted for the manufacture of a white porous earthenware, which is made into flasks and bottles, some of beautiful design and workmanship.

The city is entered from the north by a substantial stone bridge, spanning a swift but shallow river. It presents, at first sight, much more the appearance of a Spanish or Moorish town than a Persian one. The dirty brown mud huts are replaced by picturesque white houses, with coloured domes, gaily striped awnings, and carved wooden balconies overhanging the stream. Riding through the city gate, we plunge from dazzling sunshine into the cool semi-darkness of the bazaar, through which we ride for at least a quarter of an hour, when a sudden turning brings us once more into daylight in the yard of a huge caravanserai, crowded with mule and camel caravans.

The apartment or cell allotted to us was, however, so filthy that we decided to push on at once to Pasingán, the next stage, four farsakhs distant. Koom is noted for the size and venom of its scorpions; and the dim recesses of the dark, cobwebby chamber, with its greasy walls and smoke-blackened ceiling, looked just the place for these undesirable bedfellows.

So we rode on again into the open country, past crowds of beggars and dervishes at the eastern gate, as usual, busily engaged, as soon as they saw us coming, at their devotions. Clear of the city walls, one sees nothing on every side but huge storks. They are held sacred by the natives, being supposed to migrate to Mecca every year. I heard at Ispahán that, notwithstanding the outward austerity and piety of the people of Koom, there is no town in Persia where so much secret depravity and licentiousness are carried on as in the "Holy City."

The stage from Koom to Pasingán was accomplished in an incredibly short time; and I may here mention that this was the only occasion upon which, in Persia, I was ever given a fairly good horse. The word *chapar* signifies in Persian to "gallop," but it is extremely rare to find "chapar post" pony which has any notion of going out of his own pace—something between a walk and a canter, like the old grey horse that carries round the lady in pink and spangles in a travelling circus.

But to-day I got hold of a wiry, game little chestnut, who was evidently new to the job, and reached and tore away at his bridle as if he enjoyed the fun. Seeing, about half-way, that he was bleeding at the mouth, I called Gerôme's attention to the fact, and found that his horse was in the same plight—as, indeed, was every animal we passed on the road between Koom and Pasingán. This is on account of the water at and between the two places, which is full of small leeches, invisible except through a microscope. Horses, mules, and cattle suffer much in consequence, for nothing can be done to remedy the evil.

A pleasant gallop of under an hour brought us to Pasingán. It was hardly possible to realize, riding through the warm evening air, for all the world like a June evening in England, that but two days before we had well-nigh been frozen to death. Had I known what was in store for us beyond Kashán, I might have marvelled even more at this sudden and welcome change of climate.

The guest-chamber at Pasingán was already taken by a Persian khan, a rude, blustering fellow, who refused us even a corner; so we had, perforce, to make the best of it downstairs among the rats and vermin. Devoured by the latter, and unable to sleep, we rose at the first streak of dawn, saddled two of the khan's horses, and rode away to Sin-Sin before any one was astir. The poor Shagird, whom we had to threaten with a severe chastisement if he did not accompany us, was in a terrible state. The bow-string was the least he could expect when the khan came to know of the trick we had played him. An extra kerán at Sin-Sin, however, soon consoled our guide. He probably never returned to Pasingán at all, but sought his fortunes elsewhere. Persian post-boys are not particular.

Kashán is distant about fifty-two English miles from Pasingán, and lies southeast of the latter. The caravan track passes a level tract of country, sparsely cultivated by means of irrigation. Persian soil is evidently of the kind that, "tickled with a hoe, laughs with a harvest." Even in this sterile desert, covered for the most part with white salt deposits, the little oases of grain and garden looked as fresh and green as though they had been on the banks of a lake or river. But the green patches were very few and far between, and, half-way between the post-stations, ceased altogether. Nothing was then visible but a waste of brown mud and yellow sand, cut clear and distinct against the blue sky-line on the horizon. It is strange, when crossing such tracts of country, to note how near to one everything seems. Objects six or eight miles off, looked to-day as if you could gallop up to them in five minutes; and the peak of Demavend, on which we were now looking our last, seemed about twenty miles off, instead of over one hundred and fifty.

Kashán was reached on the 7th of February. At Nasirabád, a village a few miles out of the city, there had been an earthquake that morning. Many of the mud houses were in ruins, and their late owners sitting dejectedly on the remains. Earthquakes are common enough in Persia, and this was by no means our last experience in that line. Commiserating with the homeless ones, we divided a few keráns among them, in return for which they brought us large water-melons (for which Nasirabád is celebrated), deliciously flavoured, and as cold as ice.

Kashán, which stands on a vast plain about two thousand feet above sea-level, is picturesque and unusually clean for an Eastern town. The bazaar is a long one, and its numerous caravanserais finer even than those of the capital. The manufacture of silk[20] and copperware is extensive; but, as usual, one saw little in the shops, *en evidence* , but shoddy cloth and Manchester goods, and looked in vain for real Oriental stuffs and carpets. I often wondered where on earth they *were* to be got, for the most persistent efforts failed to produce the real thing. I often passed, on the road, camel and mule-cloths that made my mouth water, so old were their texture and delicate their pattern and colouring, but the owners invariably declined, under any circumstances, to part with them.

Kashán will ever be associated in my mind with the fact that I there saw the prettiest woman it was my luck to meet in Persia. The glimpse was but a momentary one, but amply sufficed to convince me that those who say that *all* Persian women are ugly (as many do) know nothing whatever about it.

It was towards sunset, in one of the caravanserais, to which, hot and tired with the long dusty ride, I came for a quiet smoke and a cup of coffee. The sensation of absolute repose was delicious after the heat and glare, the stillness of the place unbroken save for the plash of a marble fountain, and, outside, the far-off voices of the "muezzims," calling the faithful to evening prayer. From the blue dome, with its golden stars and white tracery, the setting sun, streaming in through coloured glass, threw the softest shades of violet and ruby, emerald and amber, upon the marble pavement. The stalls around were closed for the night; all save one, a "manna"[21] shop. Its owner, a white-turbaned old Turk, and myself were the sole inmates of the caravanserai. Even my "kafedji"[22] had disappeared, though probably not without leaving instructions to his neighbour to see that I did not make off with the quaint little silver coffee-cup and nargileh.

It was here that I saw the "belle" of Kashán, and of Persia, for aught I know—a tall slim girl, dressed, not in the hideous bag-like garments usually affected by the Persian female, but soft white draperies, from beneath which peeped a pair of loose baggy trousers and tiny feet encased in gold-embroidered slippers. Invisible to her, I made every effort, from my hiding-place behind a projecting stall, to catch a glimpse of her face, but, alas! a yashmak was in the way—not the thin gauzy wisp affected by the smart ladies of Cairo and Constantinople, but a thick, impenetrable barrier of white linen, such as the peasant women of Mohammedan countries wear. Who could she be? What was she doing out unattended at this late hour?

I had almost given up all hope of seeing her features, when Fortune favoured me. As the old Turk dived into the recesses of his shop to attend to the wants of his fair customer, the latter removed her veil, revealing, as she did so, one of the sweetest and fairest faces it has ever been my good fortune to look upon. A perfectly oval face, soft delicate complexion, large dark eyes full of expression, a small

[20] Kashán silk, noted throughout Persia, is of two kinds: the one thin and light for lining garments, the other thick and heavy for divans, etc. The patterns are generally white, yellow, and green on a red ground.

[21] A natural sweetmeat like nougat, found and manufactured in Persia.

[22] Attendant.

aquiline nose, but somewhat large mouth, and the whitest and smallest of teeth. Such was the apparition before me. She could not have been more than sixteen.

I could scarcely restrain from giving vent to my admiration in speech, when the old Turk returned. In an instant the yashmak was in its place, and, with a hasty glance around, my vision of beauty was scuttling away as fast as her legs could carry her. A low musical laugh like a chime of silver bells came back to me from the dark deserted alleys of the bazaar, and I saw her no more.

The manna-seller was evidently irritated, and intimated, in dumb show, that I must leave the caravanserai at once, as he was shutting up for the night. I bought a pound or so of the sweetmeat to pacify him, and, if possible, glean some information about the fair one, but my advances were of no avail.

The history of Kashán is closely allied to that of Ispahán. The former city was founded by Sultana Zobeide, wife of the celebrated Haroun-al-Raschid. Ransacked and destroyed by the Afghans in the eighteenth century, it was again restored, or rather rebuilt, by Haji Husein Khan. Perhaps the most interesting thing the city contains is a leaning minaret which dates from the thirteenth century. It is ascended by a rickety spiral staircase. From here, not so many years ago, it was the custom to execute adulterous wives. The husband, accompanied by his relations, forced his unfaithful spouse to the top of the tower and pushed her over the side (there is no balustrade), to be dashed to pieces on stone flags about a hundred and thirty feet below.

"Pas de chance, monsieur," was Gerôme's greeting as I entered the caravanserai. "The Koudoum Pass is blocked with snow, and almost impassable. What is to be done?" Mature deliberation brought but one solution to the question: Start in the morning, and risk it. "It cannot be worse than the Kharzán, anyhow," said Gerôme, cheerfully, as we rode out of Kashán next day, past the moated mud walls, forty feet high, that at one time made this city almost impregnable. I more than once during the morning, however, doubted whether we had done right in leaving our comfortable quarters at the caravanserai to embark on this uncertain, not to say dangerous, journey.

Twenty-nine farsakhs still lay between us and Ispahán; but, once past the Khurood Pass (which lies about seven farsakhs from Kashán), all would be plain sailing. The summit of the pass is about seven thousand feet above sea-level. Its valleys are, in summer, green and fertile, but during the winter are frequently rendered impassable by the deep snow, as was now the case. Khurood itself is a village of some size and importance, built on the slope of the mountain, and here, by advice of the villagers, we rested for the night. "It will take you at least a day to get to Bideshk," said the postmaster—"that is, if you are going to attempt it."

The ride from Kashán had been pleasant enough. No snow was yet visible, save in the ravines, and the extreme summits of a chain of low rocky hills, of which we commenced the ascent a couple of hours or so after leaving Kashán. Half-way up, however, it became more difficult, the path being covered in places with a thick coating of ice—a foretaste of the pleasures before us. Towards the summit of the mountain is an artificial lake, formed by a strong dyke, or bank of stonework, which intercepts and collects the mountain-streams and melted snows—a huge reservoir, whence the water is let off to irrigate the distant low plains of Kashán, and, indeed, to supply the city itself. The waters of this lake, about fifteen feet deep, were clear as crystal, the bottom and sides being cemented.

This reservoir was constructed by order of Shah Abbas, who seems to have been one of the wisest and best rulers this unfortunate country has ever had, for he has certainly done more for his country than Nasr-oo-din or any of his stock are likely to. Pass a finer caravanserai than usual, travel a better road, cross a finer bridge, and interrogate your Shagird as to its history, and you will invariably receive the answer, "Shah Abbas." At the village of Khurood, a huge caravanserai (his work) lies in ruins, having been destroyed seven or eight years ago by an earthquake. Several persons were killed, the shock occurring at night-time, when the inmates were asleep.

The post-house at Khurood was cold, filthy, and swarmed with rats—an animal for which I have always had an especial aversion. Towards midnight a Persian gentleman arrived from Kashán—a mild, benign-looking individual, with a grey moustache and large blue spectacles. The new-comer, who spoke a little French, begged to be allowed to join us on the morrow, as he was in a hurry to get to Ispahán. Notwithstanding Gerôme's protestations, I had not the heart to refuse. He looked so miserable and helpless, and indeed was, as I discovered too late next day. Our new acquaintance then suggested sending for wine, to drink to the success of our journey. At this suggestion Gerôme woke up; and seeing that, in my case, the rats had successfully murdered sleep, I gladly agreed to anything that would make the time pass till daylight. A couple of bottles were then produced by the postmaster; but it was mawkish stuff, as sweet as syrup, and quite flavourless. Gerôme and the Persian, however, did not leave a drop, and before they had finished the second bottle were sworn friends. Although wine is forbidden by the Mohammedan faith, it is largely indulged in, in secret, by Persians of the upper class. I never met, however, a follower of the Prophet so open about it as our friend at Khurood. The wine here was from Ispahán, and cost, the Persian told us, about sixpence a quart bottle, and was, in my opinion, dear at that. Shiráz wine is perhaps the best in Persia. It is white, and, though very sweet when new, develops, if kept for three or four years, a dry nutty flavour like sherry. This, however, does not last long, but gives place in a few months to a taste unpleasantly like sweet spirits of nitre, which renders the wine undrinkable. With proper appliances the country would no doubt produce excellent vintages, but at present the production of wine in Persia is a distinct failure.

Leaving at 8 a.m., we managed to reach the summit of the Koudoum by two o'clock next day, when we halted to give the horses a rest, and get a mouthful of food. Our Persian friend had returned to Koudoum after the first half-mile, during which he managed to get three falls, for the poor man had no notion of riding or keeping a horse on its legs. He reminded one of the cockney who sat his horse with consummate ease, grace, and daring, until it moved, when he generally fell off. I was sorry for him. He was so meek and unresentful, even when mercilessly chaffed by Gerôme.

A DAY IN THE SNOW

Our greatest difficulty up till now had arisen from ice, which completely covered the steep narrow pathway up the side of the mountain, and made the ascent slippery and insecure. The snow had as yet been a couple of feet deep at most, and we had come across no drifts of any consequence. Arrived at the summit, however, we saw what we had to expect. Below us lay a narrow valley or gorge, about a mile broad, separating us from the low range of hills on the far side of which lay Bideshk. The depth of the snow we were about to make a way through was easily calculated by the telegraph-posts, which in places were covered to within two or three feet of the top. "You see, sahib," said the Shagird, pointing with his whip to a huge drift some distance to the left of the wires; "two men lying under that." The intelligence did not interest me in the least. Could we or not get over this "Valley of Death"? was the only question my mind was at that moment capable of considering.

In less than a quarter of an hour we were in the thick of it, up to our waists in the snow, and pulling, rather than leading, our horses after us. It reminded me of a bad channel passage from Folkestone to Boulogne, and took about the same time—two hours, although the actual distance was under a mile and a half. Gerôme led the way as long as he was able, but, about half-way across, repeated and violent falls had so exhausted his horse that we were obliged to halt while I took his place, by no means an easy one. During this stage of the proceedings we could scarcely see one another for the steam and vapour arising from the poor brutes, whose neighs of terror, as they blundered into a deeper drift than usual, were pitiful to hear. More than once Gerôme's pony fell utterly exhausted and helpless, and it took our united efforts to get him on his legs again; while the Shagird and I left our ponies prone on their sides, only too glad of a temporary respite from their labours. If there is anything in the Mohammedan religion, the Shagird was undoubtedly useful. He never ceased calling upon "Allah!" for help for more than ten consecutive seconds the whole way across. At four o'clock we rode into the post-house at Bideshk, thoroughly done up, and wet through with snow and perspiration, but safe, and determined, if horses were procurable, to push on at once to Murchakhar, from whence two easy stages of six and three farsakhs would land us next day at Ispahán.

It was dusk, and we had just secured the only horses available, when two Armenians, bound for Teherán, rode into the yard. When told they were just too late for a relay, the rage of one of them—a short, apoplectic-looking little man—was awful to behold. As I mounted, his companion came up and politely advised us not to attempt to ride to Murchakhar by night. "The road swarms with footpads," he said, in a mysterious undertone; "you run a very great risk of being robbed and murdered if you go on to-night." "You would have run a far greater of being frozen to death, if we had not saved you by taking these horses," cried Gerôme, as we rode coolly out of the gateway.

Bideshk is noted for a great battle fought in its vicinity between the army of Nadir Shah and Ashraf the Afghan. Its post-house is also noted, as I can vouch for, for the largest and most venomous bugs between Teherán and Ispahán. We only remained there three hours, and felt the effects for days afterwards.

All trace of ice and snow disappeared a few farsakhs from here, and we galloped gaily across a hard and level plain to our destination for the night. The post-house was a blaze of light. A couple of armed sentries stood in front of the doorway, and a motley crowd of soldiers, Shagird-chapars, and peasants outside.

"You cannot come in," said the post-master, full of importance. "The Zil-i-Sultan is here on a hunting expedition. He will start away early in the morning, and then you can have the guest-room, but not before." Too tired to mind much—indeed, half asleep already—we groped our way to the stables, where, on the cleanest bundle of straw I have ever seen—or smelt, for it was pitch dark—in a Persian post-stable (probably the property of his Highness the Governor of Ispahán), we were soon in the land of dreams. Had we known that we were calmly reposing within a couple of feet of the royal charger's heels, our slumbers might not have been so refreshing. Daylight disclosed the fact.

The governor and his suite had apparently made a night of it. Although it was past eight o'clock when we made a start, the prince, his suite, soldiers, and grooms were none of them stirring, although his *chef* was busily engaged, with his staff of assistants, preparing a sumptuous breakfast of kababs, roast meat and poultry, pastry, and confectionery of various kinds. I could not help envying the man whose appetite and digestion would enable him to sit down to such a meal at such an hour. Sherbet, the Shagird from Murchakhar informed us in confidence, is the favourite drink of the Zil-i-Sultan. I only once tasted sherbet in Persia, and was somewhat surprised—so lasting are one's youthful associations—to find it utterly different to the refreshing but somewhat depressing beverage of my school-days, sold, if I remember rightly, at twopence a packet. The real sherbet I was given (in a native house at Shiráz) consisted simply of a glass of cold water with a lump of sugar in it—*eau sucré,* in fact. But Persian sherbets are of endless varieties and flavours. Preserved syrups of raspberry and pineapple, the juice of the fresh fruit of lemon, orange, and pomegranate, are all used in the manufacture of sherbet, which is, however, never effervescing. The water in which it is mixed should be icy cold, and has, when served in Persia, blocks of frozen snow floating on the surface. The "sherbet-i-bidmishk," or "willow-flower sherbet," made from flowers of a particular kind of willow distilled in water, is perhaps the most popular of all among the higher classes, and is the most expensive.

The hunting-expedition (the Shagird, who was of a communicative disposition, informed us) consisted of three parties located at villages each within a couple of farsakhs of Murchakhar. Numbering altogether over six hundred men (all mounted), they had been out from Ispahán nearly ten days. Yesterday the prince's party had been exceptionally lucky, and had had splendid sport. We passed, on the road to Géz, a caravan of fifteen mules laden with the spoil—ibex, deer, wild sheep, and even a wild ass among the slain. The latter had fallen to the governor's own rifle. There is plenty of sport to be had in Persia, if you only take the trouble to look for it, and in comparative comfort too, with tents, stores, cooking apparatus, etc., if time is no object. The country swarms with wild animals—tiger, bear, and leopard in the forests by the Caspian Sea; wild asses, jackals, and wolves in the desert regions; deer and wild goats in the mountainous districts; and, as we afterwards had uncomfortable proof, lions in the southern provinces. There is no permission needed. A European may shoot over any country he pleases, with the exception of the Shah's private preserves around Teherán. His Imperial Majesty is very tetchy on this point.

We galloped nearly the whole of the short stage from Géz to Ispahán. A couple of miles out of the city we overtook a donkey ridden by two peasants, heavy men, who challenged us to a trial of speed. We only just beat them by a couple of lengths at the gates, although our horses were fresh and by no means slow. The Persian donkey is unquestionably the best in the East, and is not only speedy, but as strong as a horse. We frequently passed one of these useful beasts carrying a whole family—monsieur, madame, and an unlimited number of bebés—to say nothing of heavy baggage, in one of the queer-looking arrangements (oblong boxes with a canvas covering stretched over a wooden framework) depicted on the next page. An ordinary animal costs from two to three pounds (English), but a white one, the favourite mount of women and priests, will often fetch as much as ten or fifteen.

A FAMILY PARTY

To reach Djulfa, the Armenian and European quarter of Ispahán, the latter city must be crossed, also the great stone bridge spanning the "Zandarood," or "Living River," so called from the supposed excellence of its water for drinking purposes, and its powers of prolonging life. Nearing the bridge, we met a large funeral, evidently that of a person of high position, from the costly shawls which covered the bier.

As in many Eastern countries, a man is never allowed to die in peace in Persia. It is a ceremony like marriage or burial, and as soon as the doctors have pronounced a case hopeless, the friends and relations of the sick man crowd into his chamber and make themselves thoroughly at home, drinking tea and sherbet, and watching, through the smoke of many hubble-bubbles, the dying agonies of their friend. The wife of the dying man sits at his side, occasionally holding to the nostrils the Persian substitute for smelling-salts, i. e. a piece of mud torn from the wall of the dwelling and moistened with cold water. As a last resource, a fowl is often killed and placed, warm and bleeding, on the patient's feet. This being of no avail, and death having taken place, the wife is led from the apartment, and the preparations for interment are commenced. Wet cotton-wool is stuffed into the mouth, nose, and ears of the corpse, while all present witness aloud that the dead man was a good and true Mohammedan. The body is laid out, a cup of water is placed at its head, and a moollah, ascending to the roof of the house, reads in a shrill nasal tone verses from the Korán. The professional mourners then arrive, and night or day is made hideous with their cries, while the "washers of the dead" proceed with their work. The coffin,[23] in Persia, is made of very thin wood; in the case of a poor man it is often dispensed with altogether, the corpse being buried in a shroud. Interment in most cases takes place forty-eight hours at most after death.

We found the house of Mr. P——, the Telegraph Superintendent of the Indo-European Company, with some difficulty, for the roads or rather lanes of Djulfa are tortuous and confusing. Mr. P——was out, but had left ample directions for our entertainment. A refreshing tub, followed by a delicious curry, washed down with iced pale ale, prepared one for the good cigar and siesta that followed, though an unlimited supply of English newspapers, the *Times, Truth,* and *Punch,* kept me well awake till the return of my host at sunset.

[23] In the north of Persia the dead are buried in a shroud of dark-blue cloth, which is, oddly enough, called in the Persian language, a *kaffin*.

CHAPTER VII.

ISPAHÁN—SHIRÁZ.

The seven telegraph-stations, in charge of Europeans, between Teherán and Bushire, may be called the oases of Persia to the weary traveller from Résht to the Persian Gulf. He is sure, at any of these, of a hearty welcome, a comfortable bedroom, and a well-cooked dinner from the good Samaritan in charge. The latter is generally the best of company, full of anecdote and information about the country, and, necessarily, well posted in the latest news from Europe, from the last Parliamentary debate to the winner of the Derby. These officials are usually *ci-devant* non-commissioned officers of Royal Engineers. Some are married, for the life is a lonely one, and three or four months often elapse without personal communication with the outer world, except on the wires. By this means, when the latter are not in public use, the telegraphist can lighten his weary hours by animated conversation with his colleague two or three hundred miles away on congenial topics—the state of the weather, rate of exchange, chances of promotion, and so on. Living, moreover, at most of the stations is good and cheap; there is plenty of sport; and if a young unmarried man only keeps clear of the attractions of the fair sex, he soon makes friends among the natives. Love intrigues are dangerous in Persia. They once led to the massacre of the whole of the Russian Legation at Teherán.

Ispahán is a city of ruins. A Persian will tell you, with pride, that it is nearly fifteen miles in circumference, but a third of this consists of heaps of stones, with merely the foundation-lines around to show that they were once palaces or more modest habitations. Chardin the traveller, writing in A.D. 1667, gives the population of Ispahán at considerably over a million, but it does not now exceed fifty thousand, including the suburb of Djulfa. The Madrassa, or College, the governor's palace, and "Chil Situn," or "Palace of the Forty Pillars," are the only buildings that still retain some traces of their former glory. Pertaining to the former is a dome of the most exquisite tile-work, which, partly broken away, discloses the mud underneath; a pair of massive gates of solid silver, beautifully carved and embossed; a large shady and well-kept garden in the centre of the Madrassa, with huge marble tanks of water, surrounded by an oblong arcade of students' rooms—sixty queer little boxes about ten feet by six, their walls covered with arabesques of great beauty. These are still to be seen—and remembered. With the exception of the "Maidan Shah," or "Square of the King"—a large open space in the centre of the city, surrounded by modern two-storied houses—the streets of Ispahán are narrow, dirty, and ill-paved, and its bazaar, which adjoins the Maidan Shah, very inferior in every way to those of Teherán or Shiráz.

The palace of "Chil Situn," or "The Forty Pillars," is like most Persian palaces—the same walled gardens with straight walks, the usual avenues of cypress trees, and the inevitable tank of stone or marble in the centre of the grounds. It is owing to the reflection of the *façade* of the palace in one of the latter that it has gained its name. There are in reality but twenty pillars, the forty being (with a stretch of imagination) made up by reflection in the dull and somewhat dirty pool of water at their feet. The palace itself is a tawdry, gimcrack-looking edifice, all looking-glass and vermilion and green paint in the worst possible taste. From the entrance-hall an arched doorway leads into the principal apartment, a lofty chamber about ninety feet long by fifty broad, its walls covered with large paintings representing the acts of the various Persian kings. Shah Abbas is portrayed under several conditions. In one scene he is surrounded by a band of drunken companions and dancing-girls, in costumes and positions that would hardly pass muster before our Lord Chamberlain. This room once contained the most beautiful and costly carpet in all Persia, but it has lately been sold "for the good of the State," and a dirty green drugget laid down in its place. In one of the side chambers are pictures representing ladies and gentlemen in the costume of Queen Elizabeth's time. How they got to Ispahán I was unable to discover. They are very old, and evidently by good masters.

The way back to our comfortable quarters at Djulfa lay over the Zandarood river. There are five bridges, the principal one being that of Allaverdi Khan, named after one of the generals of Shah Abbas, who superintended its construction. It is of solid stonework, and built in thirty-three arches, over which are ninety-nine smaller arches above the roadway on both sides, enclosing a covered-in pathway for foot-passengers. The roadway in the centre, thirty feet wide, is well paved with stone, and perfectly level. Every thirty yards or so are stalls for the sale of kababs, fruit, sweetmeats, and the kalyan, for a whiff from which passers-by pay a small sum. Ispahán is noted for its fruit; apricots, peaches, nectarines, cherries, mulberries, and particularly fine melons, are abundant in their season. There is a saying in Persia, "Shiráz for wine, Yèzd for women, but Ispahán for melons."

Since it has ceased to be the capital of Persia, the trade of Ispahán has sadly deteriorated. There is still, however, a brisk trade in opium and tobacco. Silks and satins are also made, as well as quantities of a coarser kind of cotton stuff for wearing-apparel, much used by the natives. The sword-blades manufactured here are, in comparison with those of Khorassan or Damascus, of little value. Genuine old blades from the latter city fetch enormous prices everywhere; but a large quantity of worthless imitations is in the market, and unless a stranger is thoroughly experienced in the art of weapon-buying, he had better leave it alone in Persia. Modern firearms are rarely seen in the bazaars, except cheap German and French muzzle-loaders, more dangerous to the shooter than to the object aimed at.

If the streets of Ispahán are narrow, those of Djulfa, the Armenian settlement, can only be described as almost impassable, for, although the widest are barely ten feet across, quite a third of this space is taken up by the deep ditch, or drain, lined with trees, by which all are divided. But the town, or settlement, is as clean and well-kept as Ispahán itself is the reverse, which is saying a great deal.

Djulfa is called after the Armenian town of that name in Georgia, the population of which, for commercial reasons, was removed to this place by Shah Abbas in A.D. 1603. Djulfa, near Ispahán, was once a large and flourishing city, with as many as twenty district parishes, and a population of sixty thousand souls, now dwindled down to a little over two thousand, the greater part of whom live in great want and poverty. The city once possessed as many as twenty churches, but most of these are now in ruins. The cathedral, however, is still standing, and in fair preservation. It dates from A.D. 1655. There is also a Roman Catholic colony and church. The latter stands in a large garden, celebrated for its quinces and apricots. Lastly, the English Church Missionary Society have an establishment here under the direction of the Rev. Dr. Bruce, whose good deeds during the famine are not likely to be forgotten by the people of Ispahán and Djulfa, whatever their creed or religion. The trade of Djulfa is insignificant, although there is a large amount of wine and arak manufactured there, and sold "under the rose" to the Ispahánis. The production of the juice of the grape is somewhat primitive. During the season (September and October) the grapes are trodden out in a large earthenware pan, and the whole crushed mass, juice and all, is stowed away in a jar holding from twenty to thirty gallons, a small quantity of water being added to it. In a few days fermentation commences. The mass is then stirred up every morning and evening with sticks for ten or twenty days. About this period the refuse sinks to the bottom of the jar, and the wine is drawn off and bottled. In forty days, at most, it is fit to drink.

My time at Ispahán was limited, so much so that I was not able to pay a visit to the "Shaking minarets," about six miles off. These mud towers, of from twenty to thirty feet high, are so constructed that a person, standing on the roof of the building between the two, can, by a slight movement of his feet, cause them to vibrate.

I spent most of my time, as usual, strolling about the least-frequented parts of the city, or in the cool, picturesque gardens of the Madrassa. The people of Teherán, and other Persian cities, are generally civil to strangers; but at Ispahán the prejudice against Europeans is very strong, and I more than once had to make a somewhat hasty exit from some of the lower quarters of the city.

Mrs. S——, the wife of a telegraph official, was stabbed by some miscreants while walking in broad daylight on the outskirts of the town, a few months before my visit. The offenders were never caught; probably, as Ispahán is under the jurisdiction of the Zil-i-Sultan, were never meant to be.

The Zil-i-Sultan returned to Ispahán before I left. He is rightly named "Shadow of the King," for, saving his somewhat more youthful appearance, he is as like Nasr-oo-din as two peas. Like his father in most of his tastes, his favourite occupations are riding, the chase, and shooting at a mark; but he is, perhaps, more susceptible to the charms of the fair sex than his august parent.

The prince is now nearly forty years of age. His wife, daughter of a former Prime Minister of Persia, who was strangled by order of the present Shah, died a few years ago, having borne him a son, the "Jelal-u-dowleh," a bright, clever boy, now about eighteen years old, and three daughters. The Zil-i-Sultan is adored by his people, and has, unquestionably, very great influence over the districts of which he is governor. Within the last two years, however, at least two-thirds of his possessions have been taken from him—a proceeding that caused him considerable annoyance, and drew forth the remark that the Valliad would one day regret it. There can be little doubt that, at the death of Nasr-oo-din, the Governor of Ispahán will make a bold bid for the throne; in fact, the latter makes no secret of his intentions. Drink and debauch having already rendered his younger brother half-witted, the task should not be a difficult one, especially as half the people and the whole army side with the illegitimate, though more popular, prince. It is, perhaps, under the circumstances, to be regretted that the latter is an ardent Russophile, ever since his Majesty the Czar sent a special mission to Ispahán to confer upon him the Order of the Black Eagle. Should the Zil-i-Sultan succeed Nasr-oo-din, British influence in Persia may become even less powerful than it is now, if that is possible.

The Zil-i-Sultan is far more civilized in his habits and mode of life than the Shah. A fair French scholar, he regularly peruses his *Temps, Gil Blas*, and the latest works of the best French authors. It is strange that, with all his common sense and sterling qualities, this prince should, in some matters, be a perfect child. One of his whims is dress. Suits of clothes, shirts, socks, hats, and uniforms are continually pouring in from all parts of Europe, many of the latter anything but becoming to the fat, podgy figure of the "King's Shadow." A photograph of his Royal Highness the Duke of Connaught in Rifle Brigade uniform was shown him a couple of years since. The Court tailor was at once sent for. "I must have this; make it at once," was the command, the humble request to be allowed to take the measure being met by, "Son of a hell-burnt father! What do you mean? Make it for a well-made man—a man with a better figure than that, and it will fit me!"

Popular as he is with the lower orders, the Zil-i-Sultan does not, when offenders are brought before him, err on the side of mercy. Persian justice is short, sharp, and severe, and a man who commits a crime in the morning, may be minus his head before sunset. Although a Persian would indignantly deny it, some of their punishments are nearly as cruel as the Chinese. For instance, not so very long ago a man in Southern Persia was convicted of incest, for which crime his eyes were first torn out with pincers, and his teeth then extracted, one by one, sharpened to a point, and hammered, like nails, through the top of his skull. It should be said in justice that the present Shah has done all he can to stop the torture system, and confine the death-sentence to one of two methods—painless and instantaneous—throat-cutting and blowing from a gun. Notwithstanding, executions such as the one I have mentioned are common enough in remote districts, and crucifixion, walling up, or burying and burning alive are, although less common than formerly, by no means out of date. Women are usually put to death by being strangled, thrown from a precipice or well, or wrapped up in a carpet and jumped upon; but the execution of a woman is now, fortunately, rare in Persia.

A dreary desert surrounds Ispahán on every side save to the southward, where dark masses of rock, a thousand feet high, break the sky-line. The environs of the city are well populated, and, as we rode out, *en route* for Shiráz, we passed through a good deal of cultivated land. This is irrigated by the Zandarood, whose blue waters are visible for a long distance winding through the emerald-green plain, with its gay patchwork of white and scarlet poppy-gardens. The cultivation of this plant is yearly increasing in Persia, for there is an enormous demand for the drug in the country itself, to say nothing of the export market, the value of which, in 1871, was 696,000 rupees. In 1881 it had progressed to 8,470,000 rupees, and is steadily increasing every year. Opium is not smoked in Persia, but is taken in the form of pills. Many among the upper classes take it daily, the dose being a grain to a grain and a half.

We covered, the first day out from Ispahán, nearly a hundred miles between sunrise and 10 p.m.—not bad work for Persia. A little after dark, and before the moon had risen, I was cantering easily along in front of Gerôme, when a violent blow on the chest, followed by another between the eyes, sent me reeling off my horse on to the sand. My first thought, on collecting myself, was "Robbers!"—this part of the road bearing an unpleasant reputation. Cocking my revolver, I called to Gerôme, and was answered by a volley of oaths, while another riderless horse galloped past me and disappeared in the darkness. Our foe was a harmless one. The wind had blown down one of the telegraph-posts, and the wires had done the mischief. By good luck and the aid of lucifer matches, we managed to trace our ponies to a piece of cultivated ground hard by, where we found them calmly feeding in a field of standing corn.

The moon had risen by nine o'clock. Before half-past we were in sight of the rock on which stands the town of Yezdi-Ghazt, towering, shadowy and indistinct, over the moonlit plain. This is unquestionably the most curious and interesting village between Résht and Bushire. The post-house stands at the foot. As we rode to the latter through the semi-darkness caused by the shadow of the huge mass of boulders and mud on which the town is situated, the effect was extraordinary. It was like a picture by Gustave Doré; and, looking up the dark perpendicular side of the rock at the weird city with its white houses, queer-shaped balconies, and striped awnings, standing out clear and distinct against the starlit sky, gave one an uncomfortable, uncanny feeling, hard to shake off, and heightened by the fact that, although the hour was yet early, not a light was visible, not a sound to be heard. It was like a city of the dead.

Daylight does not improve the appearance of Yezdi-Ghazt. The city, which looks so weird and romantic by moonlight, loses much of its beauty, though not its interest, when seen by the broad light of day. The system of drainage in Yezdi-Ghazt is simple, the sewage being thrown over, to fall, haphazard, on the ground immediately below. I nearly had a practical illustration during my examination, which, however, did not last long, for the side of the rock glistened with the filth of years, and the stench and flies were unbearable.

Early next morning I set out alone to explore the strange place, and with much difficulty and some apprehension—for I did not know how the natives were disposed—ascended a steep rocky path, at the summit of which a wooden drawbridge leads over a deep abyss to the gate of the city. This bridge is the only access to Yezdi-Ghazt, which is, so to speak, a regular fortress-town.

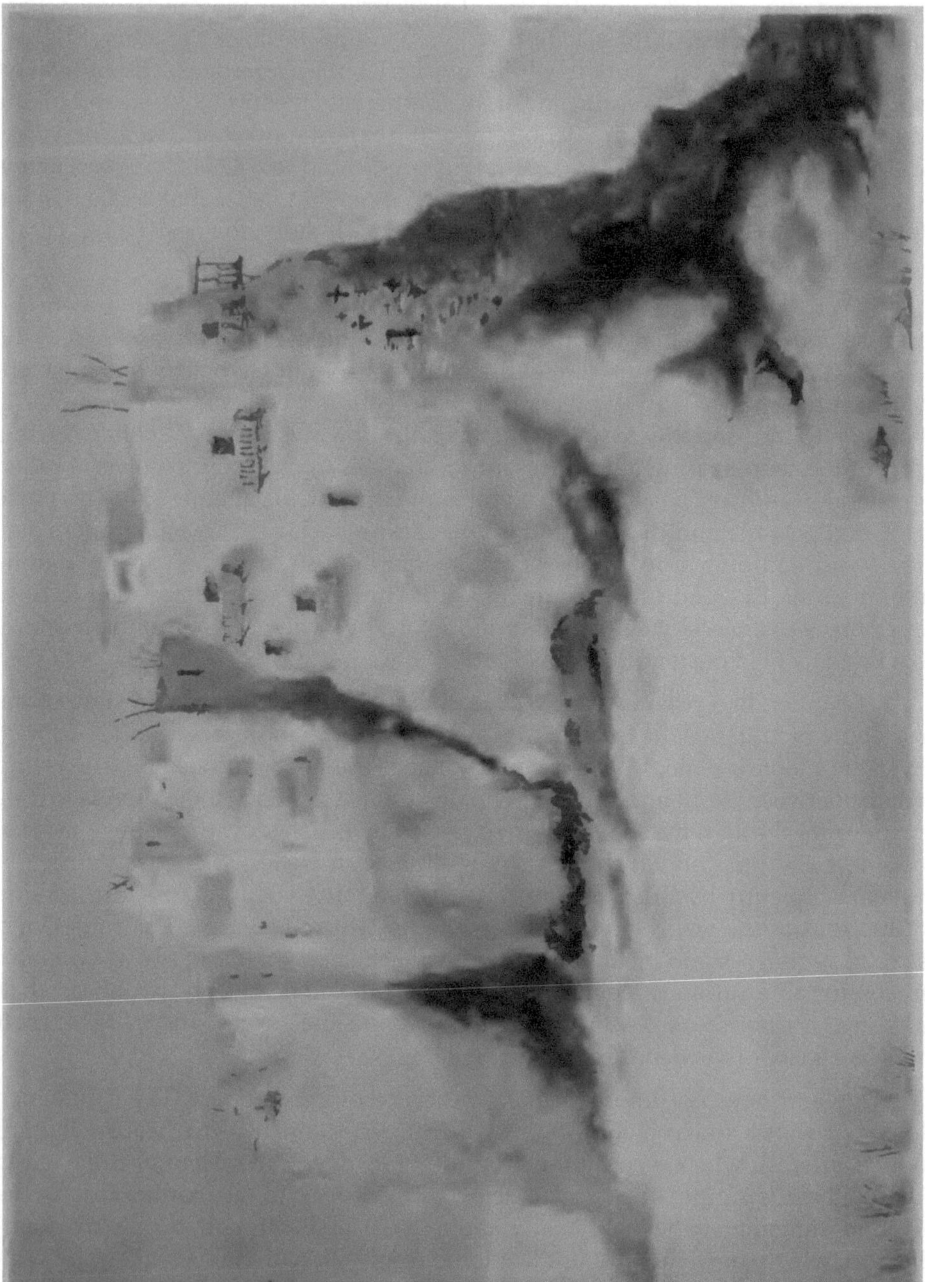

YEZDI-GHAZT

The rock, about half a mile long, is intersected by one narrow street, which, covered from end to end with awnings and wooden beams, was almost in obscurity. The sudden change from the glare outside almost blinded one. The appearance of a Farangi is evidently rare in Yezdi-Ghazt, for I was immediately surrounded by a crowd, who, however, were evidently inclined to be friendly, and escorted me to the house of the head-man, under whose guidance I visited the city.

The houses are of stone, two-storied, and mortised into the rock, which gives them the appearance, from below, as if a touch would send them toppling over, while a curious feature is that none of their windows looks inwards to the street—all are in the outside wall facing the desert. I took coffee with the head-man on his balcony—a wooden construction, projecting over a dizzy height, and supported by a couple of rickety-looking beams. It was nervous work, for the flooring, which was rotten and broken into great holes, creaked ominously. I could see Gerôme (who had evidently missed me) bustling about the post-house, and reduced, from this height, to the size of a fly. Making this my excuse, I quickly finished my coffee, and bade my host farewell, nor was I sorry to be once more safe on *terra firma.*

Yezdi-Ghazt, which has a population of about five hundred, is very old, and is said to have existed long previous to the Mohammedan conquest. The present population are a continual source of dread to the neighbouring towns and villages, on account of their lawlessness and thieving proclivities, and mix very little with any of their neighbours, who have given the unsavoury city the Turkish nickname of "Pokloo Kalla," or "Filth Castle." Yezdi-Ghazt would not be a desirable residence during an earthquake. The latter are of frequent occurrence round here. Many of the villages have been laid in ruins, but, curiously enough, the rock-city has, up till now, never even felt a shock.

A ride of under fifty miles through level and fertile country brought us to Abadéh, a pretty village standing in the midst of gardens and vineyards, enclosed by high mud walls. A European telegraph official, Mr. G——, resides here. As we passed his house—a neat white stone building easily distinguishable among the brown mud huts—a native servant stopped us. His master would not be back till sunset, but had left directions that we were to be well cared for till his return. The temptation of a bed and dinner were too much, and, as time was no object, and snowy passes things of the past, we halted for the night.

An hour later, comfortably settled on Mr. G——'s sofa, and dozing over a cigar and a volume of *Punch,* my rest was suddenly disturbed by a loud bang at the sitting-room door, which, flying open, admitted two enormous animals, which I at first took for dogs. Both made at once for my sofa, and, while the larger one curled comfortably round my feet and quietly composed itself for sleep, the smaller, evidently of a more affectionate disposition, seated itself on the floor, and commenced licking my face and hands—an operation which, had I dared, I should strongly have resented. But the white gleaming teeth and cruel-looking green eyes inspired me with respect, to use no stronger term; for I had by now discovered that these domestic pets were—panthers! To my great relief, Mr. G—— entered at this juncture. "Making friends with the panthers, I see," he said pleasantly. "They are nice companionable beasts." They may have been at the time. The fact remains that, three months after my visit, the "affectionate one" half devoured a native child! The neighbourhood of Abadéh, Mr. G—— informed me, swarms with these animals. Bears, wolves, and hyenas are also common, to say nothing of jackals, which, judging from the row they made that night, must have been patrolling the streets of the village in hundreds.

A traveller starting from Teherán for Bushire is expected at every European station on the telegraph-line. "I thought you would have got here sooner," said Mr. G——. "P—— (at Ispahán) told me you were coming through quick."

The dining-room of my host at Abadéh adjoined the little instrument-chamber. Suddenly, while we were at dinner, a bell was heard, and the half-caste clerk entered. "So-and-so of Shiráz," naming an official, "wants to speak to you." "All right," replied G——. "Just tell him to wait till I've finished my cheese!"

"It's from F——," he said, a few moments later, "to say he expects you to make his house your head-quarters at Shiráz." So the stranger is passed on through this desert, but hospitable land. Persian travel would be hard indeed were it not for the ever-open doors and hospitality of the telegraph officials.

We continue our journey next day in summer weather—almost too hot, in the middle of the day, to be pleasant. Sheepskin and bourka are dispensed with, as we ride lazily along under a blazing sun through pleasant green plains of maize and barley, irrigated by babbling brooks of crystal-clear water. A few miles from Abadéh is a cave-village built into the side of a hill. From this issue a number of repulsive-looking, half-naked wretches, men and women, with dark scowling faces, and dirty masses of coarse black hair. Most are covered with skin-disease, so we push on ahead, but are caught up, for the loathsome creatures get over the ground with extraordinary speed. A handful of "sheis"[24] stops them, and we leave them swearing, struggling, and fighting for the coins in a cloud of dust. Then on again past villages nestling in groves of mulberry trees, past more vineyards, maize, and barley, and peasants in picturesque blue dress (save white, no other colour is worn in summer by the country-people) working in the fields. Their implements are rude and primitive enough. The plough is simply a sharpened stick covered with iron. The sickle is used for reaping. Threshing is done by means of an axle with thin iron wheels. If such primitive means can attain such satisfactory results, what could not modern agricultural science be made to do for Persia?

Sunset brings a cool breeze, which before nightfall develops into a cutting north-easter, and we shiver again under a bourka and heavy fur pelisse. Crossing a ridge of rock, we descend upon a white plain, dim and indistinct in the twilight. The ground crackles under our horses' feet. It is frozen snow! A light shines out before us, however, and by ten o'clock we are snug and safe for the night in the telegraph-station of Deybid.

These sudden changes of temperature make the Persian climate very trying. At this time of year, however balmy the air and bright the sunshine at midday, one must always be prepared for a sudden and extreme change after sunset. The Plain of Deybid was covered with snow at least two feet deep, the temperature must have stood at very few degrees above zero, and yet, not five hours before, we were perspiring in our shirt-sleeves.

[24] Small copper money.

"Mashallah!" exclaims Gerôme next morning, shading his eyes and looking across the dazzling white expanse. "Are we, then, never to finish with this accursed snow?" By midday, however, we are out of it, and, as we subsequently discover, for the last time.

We had up till now been singularly fortunate as regards accidents, or rather evil results from them. To-day, however, luck deserted us, for a few miles out of Deybid my right leg became so swollen that I could scarcely sit on my horse. The pain was acute, the sensation that of having been bitten by some poisonous insect. Gerôme, ever the Job's comforter, suggested a centipede, adding, "If so, you will probably have to lie up for four or five days." The look-out was not cheerful, certainly, for at Mourghab, the first stage, I had to be lifted off my horse and carried into the post-house.

With some difficulty my boot was cut off, and revealed the whole leg, below the knee, discoloured and swollen to double its size, but no sign of a wound or bite. "Blood-poisoning," says Gerôme, decidedly. "I have seen hundreds of cases in Central Asia. It generally proves fatal there," he adds consolingly; "but the Russian soldier is so badly fed." The little man seems rather disappointed at my diagnosis of my case—the effect due to a new and tight boot which I had not been able to change since leaving Ispahán. Notwithstanding, I cannot put foot to ground without excruciating pain. Spreading the rugs out on the dirty earthen floor, I make up my mind to twenty-four hours here at least. It is, perhaps, the dirtiest post-house we have seen since leaving Teherán; but moving under the present circumstances is out of the question.

The long summer day wears slowly away. Gerôme, like a true Russian, hunts up a samovar in the village, and consoles himself with innumerable glasses of tea and cigarettes, while the medicine-chest is brought into requisition, and I bathe the swollen limb unceasingly for three or four hours with Goulard's extract and water, surrounded by a ring of admiring and very dirty natives. But my efforts are in vain, for the following morning the pain is as severe, the leg as swollen as ever. Gerôme is all for applying a blister, which he says will "bring the poison out"! Another miserable day breaks, and finds me still helpless. I do not think I ever realized before how slowly time can pass, for I had not a single book, with the exception of "Propos d'Exil," by Pierre Loti, and even that delightful work is apt to pall after three complete perusals in the space of as many weeks. From sunrise to sunset I lay, prone on my back, staring up at the cobwebby, smoke-blackened rafters, while the shadows shortened and lengthened in the bright sunlit yard, the monotonous silence broken only by the deep regular snores of my companion, whose capacity for sleep was something marvellous, the clucking of poultry, and the occasional stamp or snort of a horse in the stable below. Now and again a rat would crawl out, and, emboldened by the stillness, creep close up to me, darting back into its hole with a jump and a squeal as I waved it off with hand or foot. My visitors from the village did not return to-day, which was something to be thankful for, although towards evening I should have hailed even them with delight—dirt, vermin, and all. Patience was rewarded, for next day I was able to stand, and towards evening set out for Kawamabad, twenty-four miles distant. Though still painful and almost black, all inflammation had subsided, and three days later I was able to get on a boot. "You'd have been well in half the time," insisted Gerôme, "if you had only let me apply a blister."

The road from Mourghab to Kawamabad is wild and picturesque, leading through a narrow gorge, on either side of which are precipitous cliffs of rock and forest, three or four hundred feet high. A broad, swift torrent dashes through the valley, which is about a quarter of a mile broad. In places the pathway, hewn out of the solid rock, is barely three feet wide, without guard or handrail of any kind. This part of the journey was reached at sunset, and we did not emerge on the plain beyond till after dark. Our horses were, fortunately, as active as cats, and knew their way well, for to guide them was impossible. In places one's foot actually swung over the precipice, and a false step must have sent one crashing over the side and into the roaring torrent below, which, perhaps luckily, we could only hear, not see.

The ruins of Persepolis are situated about fifty miles north-east of Shiráz, two or three miles from the main road. Signs that we were approaching the famous city were visible for some distance before we actually reached them. Not fifty yards from the post-house of Poozeh, a picturesque spot surrounded by a chain of rocky, snow-capped hills, we came upon a kind of cave, with carvings in bas-relief on its granite walls, representing figures of men and horses from eight to ten feet high, evidently of great antiquity. The desecrating hand of the British tourist had, however, left its mark in the shape of the name "J. Isaacson" cut deep into one of the slabs, considerably marring its beauty.

It is not my intention to write a description of the ruins that now mark the spot where once stood the capital of the Persian Empire. To say nothing of its having been so graphically portrayed by far more competent hands, my visit was of such short duration that I carried away but faint recollections of the famous city. The fact that it had been persistently crammed down my throat, upon every available occasion, ever since I landed in Persia, may have had something to do with the feeling of disappointment which I experienced on first sight of the ruins. It may be that, like many other things, they grow upon one. If so, the loss was mine. I cannot, however, help thinking that to any but a student of archæology, Persepolis lacks interest. The Pyramids, Pompeii, the ancient buildings of Rome and Greece, are picturesque; Persepolis is not. I noticed, however, that here, as at Poozeh, the British tourist had been busy with chisel and hammer, and, I am ashamed to add, some of the names I read are as well known in England as that of the Prince of Wales.

On the 18th of February, just before midnight, we rode into Shiráz. The approach to the city lying before us, white and still in the moonlight, through cypress-groves and sweet-smelling gardens, gave me a favourable impression, which a daylight inspection only served to increase. Shiráz is the pleasantest reminiscence I retain of the ride through Persia.

CHAPTER VIII.

SHIRÁZ—BUSHIRE.

"The gardens of pleasure where reddens the rose,
And the scent of the cedar is faint on the air."

Owen Meredith.

Shiráz stands in a plain twenty-five miles long by twelve broad, surrounded by steep and bare limestone mountains. The latter alone recall the desert waste beyond; for the Plain of Shiráz is fertile, well cultivated, and dotted over with prosperous-looking villages and gardens. Scarcely a foot of ground is wasted by the industrious inhabitants of this happy valley, save round the shores of the Denia-el-Memek, a huge salt lake some miles distant, where the sun-baked, briny soil renders cultivation of any kind impossible.

Were it not for its surroundings—the green and smiling plains of wheat, barley, and Indian corn; the clusters of pretty sunlit villages; the long cypress-avenues; and last, but not least, the quiet shady gardens, with rose and jasmine bowers, and marble fountains which have been famous from time immemorial—Shiráz would not be what it now is, the most picturesque city in Persia.

Although over four miles in circumference, the city itself has a squalid, shabby appearance, not improved by the dilapidated ramparts of dried mud which surround it. Founded A.D. 695, Shiráz reached its zenith under Kerim Khan in the middle of the eighteenth century, since when it has slowly but steadily declined to its present condition. The buildings themselves are evidence of the apathy reigning among the Shirázis. Incessant earthquakes destroy whole streets of houses, but no one takes the trouble to rebuild them, and the population was once nearly double what it now is—40,000.

There are six gates, five of which are gradually crumbling away. The sixth, or Ispahán Gate, is the only one with any attempt at architecture, and is crenellated and ornamented with blue and yellow tile-work. A mean, poor-looking bazaar, narrow tortuous streets, knee-deep in dust or mud, as the case may be, and squalid, filthy houses, form a striking contrast to the broad, well-kept avenues, gilded domes, and beautiful gardens which encircle the city. Shiráz has fifteen large mosques and several smaller ones, but the people are as fanatical as those of Teherán are the reverse. Gerôme, who had a singular capacity for getting into mischief, entered one of these places of worship, and was caught red-handed by an old moullah in charge. Half the little Russian's life having been spent among

Mohammedans, he quickly recited a few verses of the Korán in perfect Arabic, which apparently satisfied the priest, for he let him depart with his blessing. Had the trick been discovered, he would undoubtedly have been roughly treated, if not killed, for the Shirázis have an unmitigated contempt for Europeans. There are few places, too, in Asia where Jews are more persecuted than in Shiráz, although they have their own quarter, in the lowest, most poverty-stricken part of the town, and other privileges are granted them by the Government. Shortly before my visit, a whole family was tortured and put to death by a mob of infuriated Mohammedans. The latter accused them of stealing young Moslem children, and sacrificing them at their secret ceremonies.[25] Guilty or innocent of the charge, the assassins were left unpunished.

The climate of Shiráz is delicious, but dangerous. Though to a new-comer the air feels dry, pure, and exhilarating, the city is a hot-bed of disease, and has been christened the "Fever Box." Small-pox, typhus, and typhoid are never absent, and every two or three years an epidemic of cholera breaks out and carries off a fearful percentage of the inhabitants. In spring-time, during heavy rains, the plains are frequently inundated to a depth of two or three feet, and the water, stagnating and rotting under a blazing sun, produces towards nightfall a thick white mist, pregnant with miasma and the dreaded Shiráz fever which has proved fatal to so many Europeans, to say nothing of natives. Medical science is at a very low ebb in Persia; purging and bleeding are the two remedies most resorted to by the native hakim. If these fail, a dervish is called in, and writes out charms, or forms of prayer, on bits of paper, which are rolled up and swallowed like pills. Inoculation is performed by placing the patient in the same bed as another suffering from virulent small-pox. Under these circumstances, it is scarcely to be wondered at that the Shirázis die like sheep during an epidemic, and indeed at all times. Persian surgery is not much better. In cases of amputation the limb is hacked off by repeated blows of a heavy chopper. In the case of fingers or toes a razor is used, the wound being dipped into boiling oil or pitch immediately after the operation.

The office of the Indo-European Telegraph is in Shiráz, but the private dwellings of the staff are some distance outside the city. A high wall surrounds the grounds in which the latter are situated—half a dozen comfortable brick buildings, bungalow style, each with its fruit and flower garden. Looking out of my bedroom window the morning following my arrival, on the shrubberies, well-kept lawns, bright flower-beds, and lawn-tennis nets, I could scarcely realize that this was Persia; that I was not at home again, in some secluded part of the country in far-away England. Long residence in the East had evidently not changed my host Mr. F——'s ideas as to the necessity for European comforts. The cheerful, sunlit, chintz-covered bedroom, with its white furniture, blue-and-white wall-paper, and lattice windows almost hidden by rose and jasmine bushes, was a pleasant *coup d'oeil* after the grimy, bug-infested post-houses; and the luxuries of a good night's rest and subsequent shave, cold tub, and clean linen were that morning appreciated as they only can be by one who has spent many weary days in the saddle, uncombed, unshaven, and unwashed.

[25] A similar case happened not long ago in Southern Russia.

There is no regular post-road between Shiráz and Bushire, or rather Sheif, the landing-place, eight miles from the latter city. The journey is performed by mule-caravan, resting by night at the caravanserais. Under the guidance of Mr. F— —, I therefore set about procuring animals and "chalvadars," or muleteers. The task was not an easy one; for Captain T— — of the Indian Army was then in Shiráz, buying on behalf of the Government; and everything in the shape of a mule that could stand was first brought for his inspection. By good luck, however, I managed to get together half a dozen sorry-looking beasts; but they suited the purpose well enough. The price of these animals varies very much in Persia. They can be bought for as little as £4, while the best fetch as much as £60 to £80.

Those were pleasant days at Shiráz. One never tired of wandering about the outskirts of the city and through the quiet, shady gardens and "cities of the silent," as the Persians call their cemeteries; for, when the solemn stillness of the latter threatened to become depressing, there was always the green plain, alive from morning till night with movement and colour, to go back to. Early one morning, awoke by the sound of a cracked trumpet and drums, I braved the dust, and followed a Persian regiment of the line to its drill-ground. The Persian army numbers, on a peace footing, about 35,000 men, the reserve bringing it up to perhaps twice that number.

Experienced military men have said that material for the smartest soldiery in the world is to be found in Persia. If so, it would surely be the work of years to bring the untrained rabble that at present exists under discipline or order of any kind. The regiment whose evolutions or antics I witnessed at Shiráz was not in the dress of the Russian cossack or German uhlan, as at Teherán, but in the simple uniform of the Persian line—dark-blue tunic, with red piping; loose red-striped breeches of the same colour, stuffed into ragged leather gaiters; and bonnets of black sheepskin or brown felt (according to the taste of the wearer), with the brass badge of the lion and sun. All were armed with rusty flint-locks.

As regards smartness, the officers were not much better than the men, who did not appear to take the slightest notice of the words of command, but straggled about as they pleased, like a flock of sheep. Some peasants beside me were looking on. "Sons of dogs!" said one; "they are good for nothing but drunkenness and frightening women and children." There is no love lost between the army and the people in Persia—none of the enthusiasm of other countries when a regiment passes by; and no wonder. The pay of a Persian soldier is, at most, £3 a year, and he may think himself lucky if he gets a quarter of that sum. *En revanche,* the men systematically plunder and rob the wretched inhabitants of every village passed through on the march. The passage of troops is sometimes so dreaded that commanders of regiments are bribed with heavy sums by the villagers to encamp outside their walls. Troops are not the only source of anxiety to the poor fellaheen. Princes and Government officials also travel with an enormous following, mainly composed of hangers-on and riff-raff, who plunder and devastate as ruthlessly as a band of Kurd or Turkoman robbers. They are even worse than the soldiery, for the latter usually leave the women alone. Occasionally a whole village migrates to the mountains on the approach of the unwelcome guests, leaving houses and fields at their mercy.

There is probably no peasantry in the world so ground down and oppressed as the Persian. The agricultural labourer never tries to ameliorate his condition, or save up money for his old age, for the simple reason that, on becoming known to the rulers of the land, it is at once taken away from him. Though poor, however (so far as cash and valuables are concerned), the general condition of the labouring classes is not so bad as might be supposed. In a country so vast (550,000 square miles) and so thinly populated (5,000,000 in all), a small and sufficient supply of food is easily raised, especially with such prolific soil at the command of the poorest. At Shiráz, for instance, there are two harvests in the year. The seifi, sown in summer and reaped in autumn, consists of rice, cotton, Indian corn, and garden produce; the tchatvi, sown in October and November, and reaped from May till July, is exclusively wheat and barley. A quantity of fruit is also grown—grapes, oranges, and pomegranates. Shiráz is famed for the latter. The heat and dust, to say nothing of smells, prevented me from often entering the city; but I walked through the bazaar once or twice, and succeeded in purchasing some old tapestries and a prayer-carpet. The merchants here are not so reserved and secretive as those of Teherán and other cities, and are, moreover, civil enough to produce coffee and a kalyan at the conclusion of a bargain, as at Stamboul. The best tobacco for kalyan-smoking is grown round Shiráz. Some, the coarser kind, from Kazeroon and Zulfaicar, is exported to Turkey and Egypt, but the most delicate Shiráz never leaves the country. The pipe is on the same principle as the narghileh, the smoke being drawn through a vessel of water. The tube, a wooden stalk about two feet long, is changed when it becomes tainted with use; for the people of the East (unlike some in the West) like their tobacco clean.

Manufactories are trifling in comparison with what they were in former days. Where, a century since, there stood five hundred factories owned by weavers, there are now only ten, for the supply of a coarse white cotton material called "kerbas," and carpets of a cheap and common kind. Earthenware and glass is also made in small quantities, the latter only for wine-bottles and kalyan water-bowls. All the best glass is imported from Russia. A kind of mosaic work called "khatemi," much used in ornamenting boxes and pen-and-ink cases, is turned out in large quantities at Shiráz. It is pretty and effective, though some of the illustrations on the backs of mirrors, etc., are hardly fit for a drawing-room table. Caligraphy, or the art of writing, is also carried by the Shirázis to the highest degree of perfection, and they are said to be the best penmen in the East. To write really well is considered as great an accomplishment in Persia as to be a successful musician, painter, or sculptor in Europe; and a famous writer of the last century, living in Shiráz, was paid as much as five tomans for every line transcribed.

My favourite walk, after the heat of the day, was to the little cemetery where Hafiz, the Persian poet, lies at rest—a quiet, secluded spot, on the side of a hill, in a clump of dark cypress trees a gap cut through which shows the drab-coloured city, with its white minarets and gilt domes shining in the sun half a mile away. The tomb, a huge block of solid marble, brought across the desert from Yèzd, is covered with inscriptions—the titles of the poet's most celebrated works. Near it is a brick building containing chambers, where bodies are put for a year or so previous to final interment at Kermansháh or Koom. Each corpse was in a separate room—a plain whitewashed compartment, with a square brick edifice in the centre containing the body. Some of the catafalques were spread with white table-cloths, flowers, candles, fruit, and biscuits, which the friends and relations (mostly women and children) of the defunct were discussing in anything but a mournful manner. A visit to a departed one's grave is generally an excuse for a picnic in Persia.

Hard by the tomb of Hafiz is a garden, one of many of the kind around Shiráz. It is called "The Garden of the Seven Sleepers," and is much frequented in summer by Shirázis of both sexes. A small open kiosk, in shape something like a theatre proscenium, stands in the centre, its outside walls completely hidden by rose and jasmine bushes. Inside all is gold moulding, light blue, green, and vermilion. A dome of looking-glass reflects the tesselated floor. Strangely enough, this garish mixture of colour does not offend the eye, toned down as it is by the everlasting twilight shed over the mimic palace and garden by overhanging branches of cypress and yew. An expanse of smooth-shaven lawn, white beds of lily and narcissus, marble tanks bubbling over with clear, cold water, and gravelled paths winding in and out of the trees to where, a hundred yards or so distant, a sunk fence divides the garden from a piece of ground two or three acres in extent,—a perfect jungle of trees, shrubs, and flowers.

Here, from about 4 p.m. till long after sunset, you may see the Shirázi taking his rest, undisturbed save for the ripple of running water, the sighing of the breeze through the branches, and croon of the pigeons overhead. Now and again the tinkle of caravan-bells breaks in upon his meditations, or the click-click of the attendant's sandals as he crosses the tiled floor with sherbet, coffee, or kalyan; but the interruption is brief. A few moments, and silence again reigns supreme—the perfection of rest, the acme of *Dolce far niente.* From here my way usually lay homewards, through the dusky twilight, past the city gates and along the now deserted plain. A limestone hill to the south of Shiráz bears an extraordinary resemblance to the head of a man in profile. Towards sunset the likeness was startling, and the nose, chin, and mouth as delicately formed as if chiselled by the tools of a sculptor. On fine, still evenings, parties of people would sometimes sit out on the plain till long after dark, conversing, eating sweetmeats, and tea-drinking, till the stars appeared, and the white fever mist, gathering round the ramparts, hid the city from view. Shiráz has been called the "Paris of Persia," from the cheerful, sociable character of its people as compared with other Persian cities; also, perhaps, partly from the beauty and coquetry (to use no other term) of its women.

I was enabled, thanks to my host, to glean some interesting facts concerning the latter, many European ladies having, from time to time, resided in Shiráz, and, obtaining access to the "anderoon," had afterwards given Mr. F—— the benefit of their observations.

Persian women are unquestionably allowed more freedom and liberty than those of other Oriental countries. It is extremely rare, in the bazaars of Stamboul or Cairo, to see a lady of the harem unattended, but the sight is common enough in Shiráz and Ispahán. Infidelity in Persia is therefore more common in proportion to the licence allowed; though, when discovered, it is severely punished, in some cases by death. Though a few are highly educated, the majority of Persian women are ignorant, indolent, and sensual. *Mariages de convenance* are as common as in France, and have a good deal to do with the immorality and intrigue that go on in the larger cities.

An eye-witness thus describes an "anderoon," or harem, of a prince in Ispahán: "A large courtyard some thirty yards by ten in extent. All down the centre is the 'hauz,' or tank—a raised piece of ornamental water, the surface of which is about two feet above the ground. The edges are formed of huge blocks of well-wrought stone, so accurately levelled that the 'hauz' overflows all round its brink, making a pleasant sound of running water. Goldfish of large size flash in shoals in the clear tank. On either side of it are long rectangular flower-beds, sunk six inches below the surface of the court. This pavement, which consists of what we should call pantiles, is clean and perfect, and freshly sprinkled; and the sprinkling and consequent evaporation make a grateful coolness. In the flower-beds are irregular clumps of marvel of Peru, some three feet high, of varied coloured blossom, coming up irregularly in wild luxuriance. The moss-rose, too, is conspicuous, with its heavy odour; while the edging, a foot wide, is formed by thousands of bulbs of the *Narcissus poeticus*, massed together like packed figs; these, too, give out a pleasant perfume. But what strikes one most is the air of perfect repair and cleanliness of everything. No grimy walls, no soiled curtains, here; all is clean as a new pin, all is spick and span. The courtyard is shaded by orange trees covered with bloom, and the heavy odour of neroli pervades the place. Many of the last year's fruit have been left upon the trees for ornament, and hang in bright yellow clusters out of reach. A couple of widgeon sport upon the tank. All round the courtyard are rooms, the doors and windows of which are jealously closed, but as we pass we hear whispered conversations behind them, and titters of suppressed merriment."

"The interior resembles the halls of the Alhambra. A priceless carpet, surrounded by felt edgings, two inches thick and a yard wide, appears like a lovely but subdued picture artfully set in a sombre frame. In the recesses of the walls are many bouquets in vases. The one great window—a miracle of intricate carpentry, some twenty feet by twenty—blazes with a geometrical pattern of tiny pieces of glass, forming one gorgeous mosaic. Three of the sashes of this window are thrown up to admit air; the coloured glass of the top and four remaining sashes effectually shuts out excess of light."

Such is the *coup d'oeil* on entering an anderoon. With such surroundings, one would expect to find refined, if not beautiful women; but, though the latter are rare enough, the former are even rarer in Persia. The Persian woman is a grown-up child, and a very vicious one to boot. Her daily life, indeed, is not calculated to improve the health of either mind or body. Most of the time is spent in dressing and undressing, trying on clothes, painting her face, sucking sweetmeats, and smoking cigarettes till her complexion is as yellow as a guinea. Intellectual occupation or amusement of any kind is unknown in the anderoon, and the obscene conversation and habits of its inmates worse even than those of the harems of Constantinople and Cairo, which, according to all accounts, is saying a good deal. A love of cruelty, too, is shown in the Persian woman; when an execution or brutal spectacle of any kind takes place, one-third at least of the spectators is sure to consist of women. But this is, perhaps, not peculiar to Persia; witness a recent criminal trial at the Old Bailey.

It will thus be seen that sensuality is the prevalent vice of the female sex in Persia. An English-speaking Persian at Bushire told me that, with the exception of the women of the wandering Eeliaut tribes, there were few chaste wives in Persia. Although the nominal punishment for adultery is death, the law, as it stands at present, is little else than a dead letter, and, as in some more civilized countries, husbands who are fond of intrigue, do not scruple to allow their wives a similar liberty. Not half an hour's walk from the Tomb of Hafiz, at the summit of the mountain, is a deep well, so deep that no one has ever yet succeeded in sounding it. The origin of the chasm is unknown; some say it is an extinct volcano. But the smallest child in Shiráz knows the use to which it has been put from time immemorial. It is the grave of adulterous women—the Well of Death.

An execution took place about fifteen years ago, but there have been none since. Proved guilty of infidelity, the wretched woman, dressed in a long white gown, was placed on a donkey, her face to the tail, with shaven head and bared face. In front of the *cortége* marched the executioner, musicians, dancers, and abandoned women of the town. Arrived at the summit of the mountain, the victim, half dead with fright, was lifted off and carried to the edge of the yawning abyss which had entombed so many faithless wives before her. "There is but one God, and Mohammed is His Prophet," cried a moullah, while the red-robed executioner, with one spurn of his foot, sent the unconscious wretch toppling over the brink, the awe-stricken crowd peering over, watching the white wisp disappear into eternity. Although the last execution is still fresh in the minds of many, the Well has no terrors for the gay, intrigue-loving ladies of Shiráz. They make a jest of it, and their husbands jokingly threaten them with it. Times are changed indeed in Persia!

I left Shiráz with sincere regret. Apart from the interest attached to the place, I have never received a kinder or more hospitable welcome than from the little band of Englishmen who watch over the safety, and work the wires, of the Indo-European telegraph. They are under a dozen in number. With cheap horse-flesh, capital shooting, the latest books and papers from India, a good billiard-room and lawn-tennis ground, time never hangs very heavily. Living is absurdly cheap. A bachelor can do well on £6 a month, including servants. He has, of course, no house-rent to pay.

A number of square stone towers about thirty feet high, loopholed and crenelated, are visible from the caravan-track between Shiráz and Khaneh Zinián, where we rested the first night. The towers are apparently of great antiquity, and must formerly have served for purposes of defence. We lunched at the foot of one on a breezy upland, with pink and white heather growing freely around, and a brawling, tumbling mountain stream at our feet. It was like a bit of Scotland or North Wales. The tower was in a state of decay and roofless, but a wandering tribe of ragged Eeliauts had taken up their quarters inside, and watched us suspiciously through the grey smoke of a damp, spluttering peat fire. They are a queer race, these Eeliauts,[26] and have little or nothing in common with the other natives. The sight of a well-filled lunch-basket and flasks of wine (which our kind hosts had insisted on our taking) would have brought ordinary gipsies out like flies round a honey-pot, if recollections of Epsom or Henley go for anything. Not so the Eeliauts, who, stranger still, never even begged for a sheis—a self-control I rewarded by presenting the chief, a swarthy handsome fellow, in picturesque rags of bright colour, with a couple of keráns. But he never even thanked me!

THE CARAVANSERAI, MEYUN KOTAL

[26] The Eeliauts are said to be of Arab and Kurd descent.

It seemed, next morning, as if we had jumped, in a night, from early spring into midsummer. Although at daybreak the ice was thick on a pool outside the caravanserai, the sun by midday was so strong, and the heat so excessive, that we could scarcely get the mules along. The road lies through splendid scenery. Passing Dashti Arjin, or "The Plain of Wild Almonds," a kind of plateau to which the ascent is steep and difficult, one might have been in Switzerland or the Tyrol. Undulating, densely wooded hills, with a background of steep limestone cliffs, their sharp peaks, just tipped with snow, standing out crisp and clear against the cloudless sky, formed a fitting frame to the lovely picture before us; the pretty village, trees blossoming on all sides, fresh green pastures overgrown in places by masses of fern and wild flowers, and the white foaming waterfall dashing down the side of the mountain, to lose itself in the blue waters of a huge lake just visible in the plains below. The neighbourhood of the latter teems with game of all kinds—leopard, gazelle, and wild boar, partridge, duck, snipe, and quail, the latter in thousands.

A stiff climb of four hours over the Kotal Perizun brought us to the caravanserai of Meyun Kotal. Over this pass, ten miles in length, there is no path; one must find one's way as best one can through the huge rocks and boulders. Some of the latter were two to three feet in height. How the mules managed will ever be a mystery to me. We dismounted, leaving, by the chalvadar's request, our animals to look after themselves. The summit of the mountain is under two thousand feet. We reached it at four o'clock, and saw, to our relief, our resting-place for the night only three or four hundred feet below us. But it took nearly an hour to do even this short distance. The passage of the Kotal Perizun with a large caravan must be terrible work.

The caravanserai was crowded. Two large caravans had arrived that morning, and a third was hourly expected from Bushire. There was barely standing-room in the courtyard, which was crowded with wild-looking men, armed to the teeth, gaily caparisoned mules, and bales of merchandise.

The caravanserai at Meyun Kotal is one of the finest in Persia. It was built by Shah Abbas, and is entirely of stone and marble. Surrounded by walls of enormous thickness, the building is in the shape of a square. Around the latter are seventy or eighty deep arches for the use of travellers. At the back of each is a little doorway, about three feet by three, leading into a dark, windowless stone chamber, unfurnished, smoke-blackened, and dirty, but dry and weather-proof. Any one may occupy these. Should the beggar arrive first, the prince is left out in the cold, and *vice versâ*. Everybody, however, is satisfied as a rule, for there is nearly as much accommodation for guests as in a large London or Paris hotel. Behind the sleeping-rooms is stabling for five or six hundred horses, and, in the centre of the courtyard, a huge marble tank of pure running water for drinking and washing purposes. This, and fodder for the horses, is all that there was to be got in the way of refreshment. But Gerôme, with considerable forethought, had purchased bread, a fowl, and some eggs on the road, and, our room swept out and candles lit, we were soon sitting down to a comfortable meal, with a hissing samovar, the property of the caravanserai-keeper, between us.

One need sleep soundly to sleep well in a caravanserai. At sunset the mules, with loud clashing of bells, are driven into the yard from pasture, and tethered till one or two in the morning, when a start is made, and sleep is out of the question. In the interim, singing, talking, story-telling, occasionally quarrelling and fighting, go on all round the yard till nearly midnight. Tired out with the stiff climb, I fell into a delicious slumber, notwithstanding the noise, about nine o'clock, to be awakened shortly after by a soft, cold substance falling heavily, with a splash, upon my face. Striking a match, I discovered a large bat which the smoke from our fire (there was no chimney) had evidently detached from the rafters.

I purchased, the next morning before starting, a Persian dagger belonging to one of the caravan-men. He was one of the Bakhtiari, a wild and lawless tribe inhabiting a tract of country (as yet unexplored by Europeans) on the borders of Persia and Asia Minor. The blade of the dagger is purest Damascene work, the handle of fossilized ivory. On the back of the blade is engraved, in letters of inlaid gold, in Arabic characters—

"There is one God! He is Eternal!"
"Victory is nigh, O true believer!"

Connoisseurs say that the dagger is over a hundred years old. After quite an hour's haggling (during which our departure was delayed, much to Gerôme's disgust), I managed to secure it for £9 English money, although the Bakhtiari assured me that he had already sworn "by his two wives" never to part with it. I have since been offered four times the amount by a good judge of Eastern weapons.

A second pass, the Kotal Doktar, lay between us and Bushire. Though steep and slippery in places, the path is well protected, and there are no boulders to bar the way. On leaving the caravanserai, we paused to examine the second longest telegraph wire (without support) in the world. It is laid from summit to summit of two hills, and spans a valley over a mile in width.[27]

The country round Meyun Kotal is well cultivated, and we passed not only men, but women, ploughing with the odd-shaped primitive wooden ploughs peculiar to these parts. Near the foot of the pass some children were gathering and collecting acorns, which are here eaten in the form of a kind of bread by the peasantry. Seldom has Nature seemed more beautiful than on that bright cloudless morning, as we rode through sweet-scented uplands of beans and clover, meadows of deep rich grass. By the track bloomed wild flowers, violets and narcissus, shedding their fresh delicate perfume. The song of birds and hum of insects filled the air, bright butterflies flashed across our path, while the soft distant notes of a cuckoo recalled shady country lanes and the sunlit hay-fields of an English summer. It was like coming from the grave, after the sterile deserts and bleak desolate plains of Northern Persia.

There is a small square building at the northern end of the Kotal Doktar, a mud hut, in which are stationed a guard of soldiers to be of assistance in the event of robbery of caravans or travellers. Such cases are not infrequent. Upon our ap-

[27] The longest is in Cochin China, across the river Meikong, the distance from post to post being 2560 feet.

proach, three men armed with flint-locks and long iron pikes accosted us. "We are the escort," said one, apparently the leader, from the bar of rusty gold braid on his sleeve. "You cannot go on alone. It is not safe." We then learnt that a large lion had infested the caravan-track over the pass for some days, and had but yesterday attacked the mail and carried off one of the mules, the native in charge only just escaping by climbing a tree.

Persian travel is full of these little surprises or rather items of news; for one must be of a very ingenuous disposition to be surprised at anything after a journey of any length in that country. If the man had said that an ichthyosaurus or dodo barred the way, I should have believed him just as much. Gerôme sharing my opinion that the report was got up for the sake of extorting a few keráns, we soon sent our informants about their business, and calmly proceeded on our journey. Nevertheless, the Kotal Doktar would not be a pleasant place to encounter the "king of beasts," I thought. The pass consists simply of a narrow pathway four feet wide, on the one side a perpendicular wall of rock, on the other an equally sheer precipice.

"Did you come across the lion?" was Mr. J——'s first question, as we dismounted at the gate of his telegraph-station at Kazeroon. "I suppose not," he added, seeing the surprise with which I greeted his remark. "We have had three parties out from here this week, but with no luck. I just managed to get a sight of him, and that's all. He is a splendid beast."

Ignorance had indeed been bliss in our case, and I felt some compunction when I remembered how disdainfully we had treated the ragged sergeant and his men. They would have been of no use, except in the way of stop-gaps, like the babies, in cheap prints, that the Russian traveller in the sleigh throws to the wolves to occupy their attention while he urges on his mad career, a pistol in each hand and the reins in his mouth. Still, even for this purpose, they might have been useful, and were certainly worth a few keráns. I was glad not to learn the truth till we reached Kazeroon. The enjoyment of the meal of which we partook at the summit of the pass would have been somewhat damped by the feeling that at any moment a loud roar, bursting out of the silent fastnesses of the Kotal Doktar, might announce the approach of its grim tenant.

There was, after all, nothing very remarkable about the occurrence, for the southern parts of Persia are infested with wild animals of many kinds. Of this I was already aware, but not that lions were among the number.

Kazeroon is, next to Shiráz, the most important place in the province of Fars, and has a population of about 6000. Surrounded by fields of tobacco and maize, it is neatly laid out, and presents a cheerful appearance, the buildings being of white stone, instead of the everlasting baked mud and clay. Many of the courtyards were surrounded by date palms, and the people seemed more civilized and prosperous-looking than those in the villages north of Shiráz.

"So you refused the escort over the Kotal?" said J—— that evening, as we sat over our coffee and cigars in his little stone courtyard, white and cool in the moonlight, adding, with a laugh, "Well, I don't blame you. A good story was told me the other day in Shiráz *àpropos* of escorts. It happened not long ago to an Englishman who was going to Bagdad from Kermansháh through a nasty bit of country. A good many robberies with violence had occurred, and the Governor of Kermansháh insisted on providing him with an escort, at the same time arranging for a Turkish escort to meet him on the frontier and take him on to Bagdad."

"You have seen the ordinary cavalry soldier of this country. There were twelve of them and a sergeant. V— — was the only European. All went well till they reached a small hamlet near Zarna, about twenty miles from the Turkish border. It was midday. V— — was quietly breakfasting in his tent, the horses picketed, the men smoking or asleep. Suddenly the sound of firing was heard about a mile off, not sharp and loud, but slow and desultory, like the pop, pop, pop of a rifle or revolver. V— — was not in the least alarmed, but, the firing continuing for some time, he thought well at last to inquire into the matter. What was his surprise, on emerging from his tent, to find himself alone, not a trace of his companions to be seen. There were the picket-ropes, a smouldering fire, a kalyan, and the remains of a pilaff on the ground, but no men. The firing had done it. One and all had turned tail and fled. The position was not pleasant, for V— — was naturally absolutely ignorant of the road. 'They will come back,' he thought, and patiently waited. But sunset came, then night, then the stars, and still V— — was alone, utterly helpless and unable to move backwards or forwards. At sunrise a head was shoved into his tent. But it had a red fez on, not an astrakhan bonnet. It was one of the Bagdad escort. The Turks laughed heartily when they heard the story. 'It must have been us,' they said; 'we had nothing to do, and were practising with our revolvers.' In the mean time the Persians returned post haste to Kermansháh, and evinced great surprise that V— — was not with them."

"'He was the first to fly,' said the sergeant. 'I am afraid he must have lost his way, and fallen into the hands of the robbers. If so, God help him. There were more than fifty of them.'"

J— —'s anecdote was followed by many others, coffee was succeeded by cognac and seltzer, Gerôme gave us some startling Central Asian experiences, and we talked over men and things Persian far into the night, or rather morning, for it was nearly 2 a.m. when I retired to rest.

"I hope you'll sleep well," said J— —, as he led the way to a comfortable bedroom looking out on to the needle-like peaks of the Kotal Doktar, gleaming white in the moonlight. "By the way, I forgot to tell you we usually have an earthquake about sunrise, but don't let it disturb you. The shocks have been very slight lately, and it's sure not to last long," added my host, as he calmly closed the door, and left me to my slumbers.

I am not particularly nervous, but to be suddenly aroused from sleep by a loud crash, as if the house were falling about one's ears; to see, in the grey dawn, brick walls bending to and fro like reeds, floors heaving like the deck of a ship, windows rattling, doors banging, with an accompaniment of women and children screaming as if the end of the world had arrived, is calculated to give the boldest man a little anxiety. I must at any rate own to feeling a good deal when, about 6 a.m. the following morning, the above phenomena took place. As prophesied, "it" did not last long—eight or ten seconds at most, which seemed to me an hour. Not the least unpleasant sensation was a low, rumbling noise, like distant thunder, that accompanied the shock. It seemed to come from the very bowels of the earth.

"We have them every day," said J—— at breakfast, placidly, "but one soon gets used to them." My host was obliged to acknowledge reluctantly that this morning's shock was "a little sharper than usual"! It was sharp enough, Gerôme afterwards told me, to send all the people of Kazeroon running out of their houses into the street. Common as the "Zil-Zillah"[28] is in these parts, the natives are terrified whenever a shock occurs. The great Shiráz earthquake some years ago, when over a thousand lost their lives, is still fresh in their minds.

An easy ride, through a pretty and fertile country, brought us to the telegraph-station of Konar Takta, where Mr. E——, the clerk in charge, had prepared a sumptuous breakfast. But we were not destined to enjoy it. They had, said Mr. E——, experienced no less than nine severe shocks of earthquake the night before, one of which had rent the wall of his house from top to bottom. His wife and children were living in a tent in the garden, and most of the inhabitants of the village had deserted their mud huts, and rigged up temporary shanties of palm leaves in the road. "We will have breakfast, anyhow," continued our host. "You must be hungry"—leading the way into the dining-room, where a long, deep crack in the whitewashed wall showed traces of last night's disaster.

The latter had, apparently, considerably upset my host, who, throughout the meal, kept continually rising and walking to the open window and back again, in an evidently uneasy state of mind; so much so that I was about to propose an adjournment to the garden, when a diversion was created by the entrance of a servant with a dish of "Sklitch," which he had no sooner placed on the table, than he rapidly withdrew. Sklitch is peculiar to this part of Persia. It is made of a kind of moss gathered on the mountains, mixed with cream and dates, and, iced, is delicious. But scarcely had I raised the first mouthful to my lips when my host leapt out of his seat. "There it is again," he cried. "Run!" and with a bound disappeared through the window. Before I could reach it the floor was rocking so that I could scarcely keep my feet, and I was scarcely prepared for the drop of nine feet that landed me on to the flower-beds. The shock lasted quite ten seconds. Every moment I expected to see the house fall bodily over. I left poor E—— busily engaged in removing his instruments into the garden. "Another night like the last would turn my hair grey," he said, as we bade him good-bye. Truly the lot of a Persian telegraph official is not always a bed of roses.

A gradual descent of over two thousand feet leads from Konar Takta to the village of Dalaki, which is situated on a vast plain, partly cultivated, the southern extremity of which is washed by the waters of the Persian Gulf. There is a comfortable rest-house at this village, the population of which is noted as being the most fierce and lawless in Southern Persia. Rest, though undisturbed by earthquakes, was, however, almost out of the question, on account of a most abominable stench of drainage, which came on at sunset and lasted throughout the night. So over-

[28] Earthquake.

powering was it that towards 3 a.m. both Gerôme and myself were attacked by severe vomiting, and recurrence was had to the medicine-chest and large doses of brandy. One might have been sleeping over an open drain. It was not till next day that I discovered the cause—rotten naphtha, which springs in large quantities from the ground all round the village. Curiously enough, the smell is not observable in the daytime.

"We have done with the snow now, monsieur," said Gerôme, as we rode next morning through a land of green barley and cotton plains, date palms, and mimosa. On the other hand, we had come in for other annoyances, in the shape of heat, dust, and swarms of flies and mosquitoes. Nearing the sea, vegetation entirely ceases. Nothing is visible around but hard calcined plain, brown and level, lost on the horizon seaward in a series of mirages, ending northward in a chain of rocky, precipitous mountains. The bright, clear atmosphere was remarkable; objects thirty or forty miles off looking but a mile or so away. About midday an unusual sight appeared on the horizon—two Europeans, a lady and gentleman, mounted on donkeys, and attended by a chalvadar on a third, who apparently carried all the baggage of the party. Halting for a few moments, and waiving introduction, we exchanged a few words. Mr. and Mrs. D—— were on their way to Teherán, with the object of making scientific researches at Persepolis and other parts of Persia. I could not help admiring the courage of the lady, though regretting, at the same time, the task she had set herself. To inquiries of "How is the road?" I replied, "Very good," May the lie be forgiven me! It was told for a humane purpose.

Save a large herd of gazelle on the far horizon, nothing occurred to break the monotony of the journey through deep heavy sand till about 4 p.m., when a thin thread of dark blue, cutting the yellow desert and lighter sky-line, appeared before us. It was the Persian Gulf. An hour later, and Sheif, the landing-place for Bushire, was reached.

A trim steam-launch, with Union Jack floating over her stern, awaited us. She was sent by Colonel Ross, British Resident at Bushire, who kindly invited me to the Residence during my stay in the Persian port. I was not sorry, after the hot, dusty ride, to throw myself at length on the soft, luxurious cushion, and, after an excellent luncheon, to peruse the latest English papers. Skimming swiftly through the bright blue waters, we neared the white city, not sorry to have successfully accomplished the voyage so far, yet aware that the hardest part of the journey to India was yet to come.

At a distance, and seen from the harbour, Bushire is not unlike Cadiz. Its Moorish buildings, the whiteness of its houses and blueness of the sea, give it, on a fine day, a picturesque and taking appearance, speedily dissipated, how ever, on closer acquaintance; for Bushire is indescribably filthy. The streets are mere alleys seven or eight feet broad, knee-deep in dust or mud, and as irregular and puzzling to a stranger as the maze at Hampton Court.

The Persian port is cool and pleasant enough in winter-time, but in summer the stench from open drains and cesspools becomes unbearable, and Europeans (of whom there are thirty or forty) remove *en masse* to Sabsabad, a country place eight or ten miles off. The natives, in the mean time, live as best they can, and epidemics of cholera and diphtheria are of yearly occurrence. The water of Bushire producing guinea-worms (an animal that, unless rolled out of the skin with great care, breaks, rots, and forms a festering sore), supplies of it are brought in barrels from Bussorah or Mahommerah; but this is not within reach of the poorer class. Nearly every third person met in the street suffers from ophthalmia in some shape or other—the effect of the dust and glare, for there is no shade in or about the city.

The latter is built at the end of a peninsula ten miles in length and three in breadth, the portion furthest away from the town being swampy and overflowed by the sea. Most of the houses are of soft crumbling stone full of shells; some, of brick and plastered mud; but all are whitewashed, which gives the place the spurious look of cleanliness to which I have referred. The inhabitants of this "whited sepulchre" number from 25,000 to 30,000. There is a considerable trade in tobacco, attar of roses, shawls, cotton wool, etc.; but vessels drawing over ten feet cannot approach the town nearer than a distance of three miles—a great drawback in rough or squally weather.

Were it five thousand miles away, Bushire could scarcely be less like Persia than it is. It has but one characteristic in common with other cities—its ruins. Although of no antiquity, Bushire is rich in these. With this exception, it much more resembles a Moorish or Turkish city. The native population, largely mixed with Arabs, carries out the illusion, and bright-coloured garments, white "bournouses," and green turbans throng the streets, in striking contrast to the sombre, rook-like garments affected by the natives of Iran. A stranger, too, is struck by the difference in the mode of life adopted by Europeans as compared with those inhabiting other parts of the Shah's dominions. The semi-French style of Teherán and Shiráz is here superseded by the Anglo-Indian. *Déjeuner à la fourchette, vin ordinaire,* and cigarettes are unknown in this land of tiffins, pegs, and cheroots.

My recollections of Bushire are pleasant ones. The Residency is a large, rambling building, all verandahs, passages, and courtyards, faces the sea on three sides, and catches the slightest breath of air that may be stirring in hot weather. Two or three lawn-tennis courts, and a broad stone walk almost overhanging the waves, form a favourite rendezvous for Europeans in the cool of the evening. From here may be seen the Persian Navy at anchor, represented by one small gunboat, the *Persepolis*. This toy of the Shah's was built by a German firm in 1885, and cost the Government over £30,000 sterling.

She has never moved since her arrival. Her bottom is now covered with coral and shells, her screw stuck hard and fast, while the four steel Krupp guns which she mounts are rusty and useless.

My preparations for Baluchistán were soon completed. The escort furnished me by the Indian Government had been awaiting me for some days at Sonmiani, our starting-point on the coast. A telegram from Karachi, saying that men, camels, tents, and stores were ready, was the signal for our departure, and on March 7 I took leave of my host to embark on the British India Company's steamer *Purulia,* for Baluchistán. With genuine regret did I leave my pleasant quarters at the Residency. Enjoyable as my visit was, it had not come upon me quite as a surprise, for the hospitality of Colonel Ross, Resident of Bushire, is well known to travellers in Persia.

CHAPTER IX.

BALUCHISTÁN—BEÏLA.

The coast-line of Baluchistán is six hundred miles long. On it there is one tree, a sickly, stunted-looking thing, near the telegraph station of Gwádar, which serves as a landmark to native craft and a standing joke to the English sailor. Planted some years since by a European, it has lived doggedly on, to the surprise of all, in this arid soil. The Tree of Baluchistán is as well known to the mariner in the Persian Gulf as Regent Circus or the Marble Arch to the London cabman.

With this solitary exception, not a trace of vegetation exists along the sea-board from Persian to Indian frontier. Occasionally, at long intervals, a mud hut is seen, just showing that the country is inhabited, and that is all. The steep, rocky cliffs, with their sharp, spire-like summits rising almost perpendicularly out of the blue sea, are typical of the desert wastes inland.

"And this is the India they talk so much about!" says Gerôme, contemptuously, as we watch the desolate shores from the deck of the steamer. I do not correct the little man's geography. It is too hot for argument, for the heat is stifling. There is not a breath of air stirring, not a ripple on the smooth oily sea, and the sides of the ship are cracking and blistering in the fierce, blinding sunshine. Under the awning the temperature is that of a furnace, and one almost regrets the cold and snow of three weeks ago, so perverse is human nature.

Mark Tapley himself would scarcely have taken a cheerful view of things on landing at Sonmiani. Imagine a howling wilderness of rock and scrub, stretching away to where, on the far horizon, some low hills cut the brazen sky-line. On the beach the so-called town of Sonmiani—a collection of dilapidated mud huts, over which two or three tattered red and yellow banners flutter in the breeze, and beneath which a small and shallow harbour emits a powerful odour of mud, sewage, and rotten fish. Every hut is surmounted by a "badgir," or wind-catcher—a queer-looking contrivance, in shape exactly like a prompter's box, used in the summer heats to cool the interior of the dark, stifling huts. A mob of ragged, wild-looking Baluchis, with long, matted locks and gaudy rags, completes this dreary picture.

Shouts of "Kamoo!" from the crowd brought a tall, good-looking native, clad in white, out of an adjacent hut, who, I was relieved to find, was the interpreter destined to accompany us to Kelát. The camels and escort were, he said, ready for a start on the morrow, if necessary. In the mean time there was a bare but clean Government bungalow at our disposal, and in this we were soon settled. But notwithstanding the comparative comfort of our quarters compared with the filthy native houses around, I determined to get away as soon as possible. The mosquitoes were bad enough, but the flies were far worse. Ceiling, walls, and floor were black with them. One not only ate them with one's food, but they inflicted a nasty, poisonous bite. As for the smells, they were beyond description; but the fact that a dead camel was slowly decomposing in the immediate vicinity of our dwelling may have had something to do with this.

With all these drawbacks, I was glad to find the population, although dirty, decidedly friendly—rather too much so, indeed; for the little whitewashed room was crowded to overflowing the greater part of the day with relays of visitors, who apparently looked upon us as a kind of show got up for their entertainment. Towards sunset a tall, swarthy fellow, about fifty years old, with sharp, restless eyes and a huge hook nose, made his appearance at the doorway; and this was the signal for a general stampede, for my visitor was no other than the head-man of Sonmiani—Chengiz Khan.

Chengiz was attired in a very dirty white garment, loose and flowing to the heels, and a pair of gold-embroidered slippers. A small conical cap of green silk was perched rakishly on the top of his head, from which fell, below the shoulders, a tumbled mass of thick, coarse, black hair. The head-man was unarmed, but his followers, five in number, fairly bristled with daggers and pistols. Like all natives, Chengiz was at first shy and reserved. It was only when I had prevailed upon him to take a cigar that my visitor became more at his ease. Having lit his cheroot, he took a long pull and passed it on to one of his followers, who repeated the performance. When it had gone the round twice it was thrown away; and Chengiz, turning to Kamoo, gravely asked if I wished for anything before he retired for the night.

"You should reach Kelát in twenty-five days," was the answer to my question, "provided the camels keep well and you have no difficulty with the people at Gwarjak; they are not used to Europeans, and may give you some trouble."

One of the men here whispered to his chief.

"Malak is the name of the head-man at Gwarjak," went on Chengiz—"a treacherous, dangerous fellow. Do not have much to do with Malak; he detests Europeans."

Malak was, judging from my experiences that night, not the only Baluchi possessed of this failing. Chengiz having left, I retired to rest, to be suddenly aroused at midnight by a piercing yell, and to find a tall, half-naked fellow, with wild eyes and a face plastered with yellow mud, standing over me, brandishing a heavy club. Though a revolver was at hand, it was useless; for I saw at a glance that I had to deal with a madman. After a severe tussle, Gerôme and I managed to throw out the unwelcome visitor and bar the door, though we saw him for an hour or more prowling backwards and forwards in the moonlight in front of the bungalow, muttering to himself, waving his arms about, and breaking every now and then into peals of loud laughter. The incident now seems trifling enough, though it left a powerful impression upon my mind that night, on the eve of setting out through an unknown country, where the life of a European more or less is of little moment to the wild tribes of the interior. The madman was a dervish, the head-man said, and perfectly harmless as a rule, but liable to fits of rage at sight of a European and unbeliever. I was, therefore, not sorry to hear next morning that this ardent follower of the Prophet had been securely locked up, and would not be released till the morrow, when we were well on the road to Beïla.

There are, I imagine, few countries practically so little known to Europeans as the one we were about to traverse. I had, up to the time of my visit, often wondered that, with India so near, Baluchistán should have been so long allowed to remain the *terra incognita* it is. My surprise ceased on arrival at Kelát. It is impossible to conceive a more monotonous or uninteresting journey, from a traveller's point of view, than that from the sea to Quetta—a distance (by my route) of nearly five hundred miles, during which I passed (with the exception of Kelát and Beïla) but half a dozen villages worthy of the name, and met, outside the villages in question, a dozen human beings at the most. This is, perhaps, scarcely to be wondered at. The entire population of the country does not exceed 450,000, while its area is estimated at something like 140,000 square miles, of which 60,000 are under Persian rule, and the remaining 80,000 (nominally) under the suzerainty of the Khan of Kelát.

The inhabitants of Baluchistán may be roughly divided into two classes: the Brahuis[29] in the north, and the Baluchis in the south. The former ascribe their origin to the earliest Mohammedan invaders of Persia, and boast of their Arab descent; the latter are supposed by some to have been originally a nation of Tartar mountaineers who settled at a very early period in the southern parts of Asia, where they led a nomad existence for many centuries, governed by their own chiefs and laws, till at length they became incorporated and attained their present footing at Kelát and throughout Northern Baluchistán. Both races differ essentially in language and customs, and are subdivided into an infinitesimal number of smaller tribes under the command or rule of petty chiefs or khans. Although somewhat similar in appearance, the Brahuis are said to be morally and physically superior to their southern neighbours. The Baluch, as I shall now call each, is not a prepossessing type of humanity on first acquaintance, with his swarthy sullen features, dark piercing eyes, and long matted locks. Most I met in the interior looked, a little distance off, like perambulating masses of dirty rags; but all, even the filthiest and most ragged, carried a bright, sharp tulwar. Though rough and uncouth, however, I found the natives, as a rule, hospitable and kindly. It was only in the far interior that any unpleasantness was experienced. This was, perhaps, only natural, seeing that seventy miles of the journey lay through a region as yet unexplored by Europeans, the inhabitants of which were naturally resentful of what they imagined to be intrusion and interference.

[29] The traveller Masson says that the word *Brahui* is a corruption of *Ba-roh-i,* meaning literally, "of the waste."

SONMIANI

Owing to the nomadic nature of the Baluchis, the barrenness of their country, and consequent absence of manufactures and commerce, permanent settlements are very rare. With the exception of Quetta, Kelát, Beïla, and Kej, there are no towns in Baluchistán worthy of the name. Even those I have mentioned are, with the exception of Quetta (now a British settlement), mere collections of tumble-down mud huts, invariably guarded by a ramshackle fort and wall of the same material. The dwellings of the nomads consist of a number of long slender poles bent and inverted towards each other, over which are stretched slips of coarse fabrics of camel's hair. It was only in the immediate neighbourhood of Gwarjak that the native huts were constructed of dried palm-leaves, the fertile soil of that district rendering this feasible.

Attended by Chengiz Khan in a gorgeous costume of blue and yellow silk, and followed by a rabble of two or three hundred men and boys, I visited the bazaar next morning. Chengiz had preceded his visit with the present of a fine goat, and evidently meant to be friendly, informing me, before we had gone many yards, that the Queen of England had just invested the Djam of Beïla (a neighbouring chief) with the Star of India, and did I think that that honour was very likely to accrue to him?

The trade of Sonmiani is, as may be imagined, insignificant. Most of the low dark stalls were kept for the sale of grain, rice, salt, and tobacco, by Hindus; but I was told that a brisk trade is done in fish and sharks' fins; and dried fruits, madder, and saffron, sent down from the northern districts, are exported in small quantities to India and Persia. In the vicinity are some ancient pearl-fisheries of considerable value, which were once worked with great profit. These have been allowed to lie for many years undisturbed, owing to lack of vigour and enterprise on the part of those in power in the state. Here is a chance for European speculators.

By a well in the centre of the village stood some young girls and children. The former were decidedly good looking, and one, but for the hideous gold nose-ring,[30] would have been almost beautiful. Here, as elsewhere in Baluchistán, the women present much more the Egyptian type of face than the Indian—light bronze complexions, straight regular features, and large, dark, expressive eyes. None of these made the slightest attempt at concealment. As we passed, one of them even nodded and smiled at Chengiz, making good use of her eyes, and disclosing a row of small, pearly teeth. Their dress, a loose divided skirt of thin red stuff, and short jacket, with tight-fitting sleeves, open at the breast, showed off their slight graceful figures and small, well-shaped hands and feet to perfection. Chengiz, pointing to the group, smiled and addressed me in a facetious tone. "He wants to know if you think them pretty," said my interpreter; but I thought it best to maintain a dignified silence. The chief of Sonmiani was, for a Mohammedan, singularly lax.

A kind of rough pottery is made at Sonmiani, and this is the only industry. Some of the water-jars were neatly and gracefully fashioned, of a delicate grey-green colour; others red, with rude yellow devices painted on them. The clay is porous, and keeps the water deliciously cool.

[30] These rings are sometimes so heavy that they are attached to a band at the top of the head to lessen the weight on the nostril.

By four o'clock next morning all was ready for a start. The caravan consisted of eighteen camels, four Baluchis, Kamoo, and Gerôme, with an escort of ten soldiers of the Djam of Beïla, smart-looking, well-built fellows in red tunics, white baggy trousers, and dark-blue turbans. Each man, armed with a Snider rifle and twenty rounds of ammunition, was mounted on a rough, wiry-looking pony. As we were starting, Chengiz Khan rode up on a splendid camel, and announced his intention of accompanying us the first stage, one of eighteen miles, to Shekh-Raj.

Here the honest fellow bade us good-bye. "The sahib will not forget me when he gets to India," he said, on leaving, thereby implying that he wished to be well reported to the Indian Government. "But take care of Malak; he is a bad man—a very bad man."

A rough and tedious journey of two days over deep sandy desert, varied by an occasional salt marsh, brought us to Beïla, the seat of government of the Djam, or chief of the province of Las Beïla, eighty miles due north of Sonmiani. With a feeling of relief I sighted the dirty, dilapidated city, with its mud huts and tawdry pink and green banners surmounting the palace and fort. The Baluch camel is not the easiest animal in existence, and I had, for the first few hours of the march, experienced all the miseries of *mal de mer* brought on by a blazing sun and the rolling, unsteady gait of my ship of the desert. Though awkward in his paces, the Baluch camel is swift. They are small and better looking than most; nor do their coats present so much the appearance of a "doormat with the mange," as those of the animals of other countries. We had as yet passed but two villages—three or four low shapeless huts, almost hidden in rock and scrub by the side of the caravan-track, which, as far as Beïla, is pretty clearly defined. There had been nothing else to break the dull, dead monotony of sand and swamp, not a sign of human life, and but one well (at Outhal) of rather brackish water.

On the second day one of the escort had pointed out a dry rocky bed as the river Purali, which is one of the largest in Baluchistán, but, like all the others, quite dry the greater portion of the year. There are no permanent rivers in this country. To this fact is perhaps due the slight knowledge obtained up to the present time of the interior, where arid sandy deserts, dangerous alike to native or European travellers, are the rule, and cover those large open spaces marked upon maps as "unexplored." Notwithstanding the great width of the bed of the Purali river in many places, it has no regular outlet into the sea. Its waters, when in flood from rainfall, lose themselves in the level plains in a chain of lagoons or swamps. Some of these are several miles in length, but decrease considerably in the dry season, when the water becomes salt. The Habb river, which divides Las from the British province of Sind, is another case in point. It possesses permanent banks, is fed from the Pabb chain of mountains, and after heavy rains in these hills a large body of water is formed, which rushes down to the sea with great force and velocity. But at other times water is only to be found in a few small pools in its rocky bed. It is, in short, a mountain torrent on a large scale. So also with the greater number of streams in the western districts, though a few of these have more the semblance of rivers than can be found elsewhere in Baluchistán. Of lakes there are none throughout the entire area of the country.

OUR CAMP AT OUTHAL

At Outhal we were met by one Hussein Khan, a wild-looking fellow mounted on a good-looking chestnut horse, its saddle and headstalls ornamented with bright-coloured leathers and gold and silver ornaments. Hussein was from Beïla, with a message from the Djam to say that I was welcome in his dominions. Tents were then pitched, and I invited Hussein to partake of refreshment, which was refused. He accepted a cigarette, however, but seemed undecided whether to smoke or eat it, till presented with a light. Having asked if I would like to be saluted with guns on arrival, an offer I politely declined, my visitor then left to prepare for our reception on the morrow.

Daybreak saw us well *en route*, and by 10 a.m. we were in sight of Beïla. About a mile or so out of the city, a mounted sowar in scarlet and gold uniform, and armed with two huge horse-pistols and a long cavalry sabre, galloped up to the caravan. "It is a messenger from the palace," said Kamoo, "to say that his Highness the Djam has been suddenly called away to Kej,[31] but that his son, Prince Kumal Khan, is riding out in state to meet the sahib, and conduct him to his father's city."

The prince shortly afterwards appeared, mounted on a huge camel, the tail and hind quarters of which were ornamented with intricate patterns stamped on the hide by some peculiar process. A guard of honour of thirty soldiers accompanied, while a rabble of two or three hundred foot people surrounded the party, for the sight of a white face is rare in Beïla. It was a strange scene: the picturesque city, brilliant barbaric costume of the young chief and his followers, and crowd of wild, half-naked Baluchis were fitly set off by surroundings of desert landscape and dazzling sunshine. A Gerôme or Vereschágin would have revelled in the sight.

Shaking hands with Kumal (no easy matter on camels), he placed me on his right hand, and, heading the procession, we rode into Beïla, where a large tent had been erected for my accommodation. Having placed a guard at my disposal, the prince then left, announcing his intention of receiving me in state that afternoon at the palace.

Beïla, which is protected by a fort and high mud wall, is situated on the right bank of the river Purali, which, at the time of my visit, was no more than a dry rocky bed. The town contains about 4000 inhabitants, and, from a distance, presents a curious appearance, each house being fitted, as at Sonmiani, with a large "badgir," or wind-catcher. Like most Eastern cities, Beïla does not improve on closer acquaintance. The people are dirty and indolent. There is little or no trade, and the dark, narrow streets, ankle-deep in mud and filth, are crowded with beggars and pariah dogs, while the dull drab colour of the mud houses is depressing in the extreme. The fort and palace alone are built of brick, and, being whitewashed, relieve to a certain extent the melancholy aspect of the place. I was escorted to the latter the afternoon of my arrival by a guard of honour, preceded by the Djam's band—half a dozen cracked English cavalry trumpets!

Djam Ali Khan, the present ruler of the state of Las Beïla, is about fifty years of age, and is a firm ally of England. The Djam is a vassal of the Khan of Kelát, but, like most independent Baluch chiefs, only nominally so. So far as I could glean,

[31] A town in Western Baluchistán.

the court of Kelát has no influence whatsoever beyond a radius of twenty miles or so from that city. The provinces of Sarawán, Jhalawán, Kach-Gandáva, Mekrán,[32] and Las Beïla, which constitute the vast tract of country known as Kalati Baluchistán, are all governed by independent chiefs, nominally viceroys of the Khan of Kelát. Practically, however, the latter has little or no supremacy over them, nor indeed over any part of Baluchistán, Kelát and its suburbs excepted.

Prince Kumal Khan received me in his father's durbar-chamber, a cheerless, whitewashed apartment, bare of furniture save for a somewhat rickety "throne" of painted wood, and a huge white linen punkah, overlooking a dreary landscape of barren desert and mud roofs. The prince, a tall, slim young man, about twenty-five years of age, has weak but not unpleasing features. He was dressed in a close-fitting tunic of dark-blue cloth, heavily trimmed with gold braid, baggy white linen trousers, and a pair of European side-spring boots, very dirty and down at heel. A light-blue turban completed his attire.

The interview was not interesting. Notwithstanding all my efforts and the services of the interpreter, Kumal was evidently shy and ill at ease, and resolutely refused to enter into conversation. One thing, however, roused him. Hearing that I was accompanied by a Russian, Kumal eagerly demanded that he should be sent for. Gerôme presently made his appearance, and was stared at, much to his discomfiture and annoyance, as if he had been a wild beast. A pair of white-linen drawers, no socks, carpet slippers, and a thin jersey, were my faithful follower's idea of a costume suitable to the Indian climate—surmounted by the somewhat inappropriate head-dress of a huge astrakhan cap, which for no earthly consideration could he be persuaded to exchange for a turban. "So that is a Russian!" said the prince, curiously surveying him from head to foot. "I thought they were all big men!" But patience has limits, and, with a muttered "Dourák,"[33] poor Gerôme turned and left the princely presence in anything but a respectful manner.

Coffee and nargileh discussed, my host moved an adjournment to the roof of the palace, where, he said, I should obtain a better view of his father's city. This ceremony concluded, the trumpets sounded, a gentle hint that the audience was at an end, and I took leave, and returned to camp outside the walls of the town.

The Wazir, or Prime Minister, of the Djam paid me a visit in the evening *sans cérémonie*—a jolly-looking, fresh-complexioned old fellow, dressed in a suit of karki, cut European fashion, and with nothing Oriental about him save a huge white linen turban. The Wazir spoke English fairly well, and, waxing confidential over a cigar and whisky-and-water (like my Sonmiani friend, the Wazir was no strict Mussulman), entertained me with an account of the doings of the Court in Beïla and the *aventures galantes* of Kumal, who, from all accounts, was a veritable Don Juan. "Will the Russians ever take India?" asked the old fellow of Gerôme, as he left the tent. "You can tell them they shall never get it so long as *we* can prevent them;" but the next moment the poor Wazir, to Gerôme's delight, had measured

[32] The word "Mekrán" is said to be derived from "Mahi-Kharan," or "Fish-eaters," which food the inhabitants of this maritime province subsisted on in Alexander's time, and do still.

[33] Russian, "Fool."

his length on the ground. Either the night was very dark, or the whisky very strong; a tent-rope had avenged the taunt levelled at my companion's countrymen.

Early next morning came a message from Prince Kumal, inviting me to visit the caves of Shahr-Rogan, an excavated village of great antiquity, about ten miles from Beïla. I gladly accepted. The camels were tired; the men of the caravan unwilling to proceed for another day, and time hung heavily on one's hands, with nothing to vary the monotony but an occasional shot at a wood-pigeon (which swarm about Beïla), or a game of *ecarté* (for nuts) with Gerôme.

The caves were well worth a visit. I could gain no information at Beïla, Quetta, or even Karachi, as to the origin of this curious cave-city, though there can be no doubt that it is of great antiquity. Carless the traveller's account is perhaps the most authentic.

"About nine miles to the northward of Beïla a range of low hills sweeps in a semicircle from one side of the valley to the other, and forms its head. The Purali river issues from a deep ravine on the western side, and rushes down (in the wet season) about two hundred yards broad. It is bounded on one side by steep cliffs, forty or fifty feet high, on the summit of which is an ancient burial-ground. Following the stream, we gained the narrow ravine through which it flows, and, turning into one of the lateral branches, entered Shahr-Rogan."

Here, on the day in question, Prince Kumal called a halt. A couple of small tents were pitched, and a meal, consisting of an excellent curry, stewed pigeons, beer, and claret, served. Leaving the Prince to amuse himself and delight his followers with his skill in rifle-shooting at a mark chalked out on the rocks, I continued my explorations. The result is, perhaps, better explained to the reader in the words of an older and more experienced observer. Carless says—"The scene was singular. On either side of a wild broken ravine the rocks rise perpendicularly to the height of four or five hundred feet, and are excavated, as far as there is footing to ascend, up to the summit. The excavations are most numerous along the lower part of the hills, and form distinct houses, most of which are uninjured by-time. They consist, in general, of a room fifteen feet square, forming a kind of open verandah, with an interior chamber of the same dimensions, to which admittance is gained by a narrow doorway. There are niches for lamps in many, and a place built up and covered in, apparently to hold grain. Most of the houses or caves at the summits of the cliffs are now inaccessible, from the narrow precipitous paths by which they were approached having worn away. The cliffs are excavated on both sides of the valley for a distance little short of a mile. There cannot be less than fifteen hundred of these strange habitations."

The caves of Shahr-Rogan are not the only sights of interest near Beïla. Time, unfortunately, would not admit of my visiting the mud-volcanoes of Las, situated near the Harra Mountains, about sixty miles from Shahr-Rogan. The hills upon which these are found are from three to four hundred feet high, and are conical in form, with flattened and discoloured tops and precipitous sides. At their bases are numerous fissures and cavities reaching far into their interior. Captain Hart, who visited these geysers some years ago, describes them as basins of liquid mud, about a hundred paces in diameter, in a continual state of eruption. These geysers, or "chandra-kupr," as they are called by the Baluchis, are also found on parts of the Mekrân coast. Colonel Ross, H.M.'s Resident at Bushire, is of opinion that these coast craters have communication with the sea, as the state of the tides has considerable influence on the movements of the mud. This theory is, perhaps, strengthened by the fact that by the coast natives the volcanoes are called "Darya-Chân," or "Eyes of the Sea."

On the way back from Shahr-Rogan to Beïla a herd of antelope was seen. I may here mention that, with one exception, this was the only occasion upon which I came across big game of any kind throughout the journey, although, from all accounts, there is no lack of wild animals in Baluchistán. Bear and hyena are found in the southern districts, and the leopard, wolf, ibex, and tiger-cat exist in other parts of the country. The wild dog is also found in the northern and more mountainous regions. The latter hunt in packs of twenty and thirty, and will seize a bullock and kill him in a few minutes. On the other hand, vermin and venomous animals are not so common as in India. Dangerous snakes are rare, though we were much annoyed by scorpions and centipedes in the villages of the north, and a loathsome bug, the "mangar," which infests the houses of Kelát.

Riding homewards, we stopped about a mile out of Beïla to inspect the Djam's garden, a large rambling piece of ground about fifty acres in extent, enclosed by high walls of solid masonry. Never was I more surprised than upon entering the lofty iron gates guarded by a sowar in neat white uniform. It seemed incredible that such fertility and abundance could exist in this dry, arid land. The cool fragrant gardens, with their shady grass walks, forest trees, and palms, springing up, as it were, out of the scorched, stony desert, reminded one of a bunch of sweet-smelling flowers in a fever ward, and the scent of rose, jasmine, and narcissus was apparent quite half a mile away. In the centre of the garden is a tamarind tree of enormous girth. It takes twelve men with joined hands to surround it. Half an hour was spent in this pleasant oasis, which was constructed by the late Djam, after infinite trouble and expense, by means of irrigation from the Purali river. There are also two deep wells of clear water in the grounds, which are never quite dry even in the hottest seasons.

Proceeding homewards, we had scarcely reached camp when a terrific thunderstorm burst over our heads. The thunderclaps were in some instances nearly a minute in duration, and the lightning unpleasantly close and vivid.

The weather clearing, I visited the bazaar in the evening, under the guidance of my old friend, the Wazir. Trade is, as I have said, practically *nil* in Beïla, and the manufactures, which are trifling, are confined to oil, cotton, a rough kind of cloth, and coarse carpets; indeed, throughout the country, commerce is almost at a standstill.

This is scarcely surprising when the semi-savage state of the people, and consequent risks to life and property, are taken into account. The export trade of the interior is, though trifling at present, capable, under firm and wise rule, of great improvement. Madder, almonds, and dried fruit from Kelát and Mastung, seed and grain from Khozdar, small quantities of assa-foetida from Nushki, and sulphur from Kach-Gandáva, comprise all the exports. From Mekrán and Las Beïla are exported "rogan," or clarified butter used for cooking purposes, hides, tobacco (of a very coarse kind), salt fish, oil-seeds, and dates. The imports chiefly consist of rice, pepper, sugar, spices, indigo, wood, and piece goods, chiefly landed at the ports of Gwádar or Sonmiani. But little is as yet known of the mineral products of this district. Iron ore is said to exist in the mountains north of Beïla, while to the south copper is reported as being found in large quantities; but nothing has as yet been done to open up the mineral resources of the district. Although silver and even gold have been found in small quantities, and other minerals are known to exist, the only mines at present in Baluchistán are those near Khozdar, in the province of Jhalawán, where lead and antimony are worked, but in a very primitive manner.

Notwithstanding the trade stagnation, there seems to be a good deal of cultivation in and around Beïla. Water is obtained from deep wells; and vegetables, rice, and tobacco are largely grown. Most of the stalls in the bazaar were devoted to the sale of rice, wheat, and tobacco, cheap cutlery, and Manchester goods; and I noticed, with some surprise, cheap photographs of Mrs. Langtry, Ellen Terry, Miss Nelly Farren, Sylvia Grey, and other leading lights of society and art, spread out for sale among the many-bladed knives, nickel forks and spoons, and German timepieces. Although the narrow alleys reeked with poisonous smells and filth and abomination of all kinds, Beïla is not unhealthy—so at least the Wazir informed me. I doubted the truth of this assertion, however, for the features of every second person I met were scarred more or less with small-pox.

My caravan, on leaving Beïla, was considerably increased. It now consisted of twenty-two camels (six of which were laden with water), five Baluchis, my original escort, and six of the Djam's cavalry. I could well have dispensed with the latter, but the kindly little Wazir would not hear of my going without them. An addition also to our party was a queer creature, half Portuguese, half Malay, picked up by Gerôme in the Beïla bazaar, and destined to fulfil the duties of cook. How he had drifted to Beïla I never ascertained, and thought it prudent not to inquire too much into his antecedents. No one knew anything about him, and as he talked a language peculiar to himself, no one was ever likely to; but he was an undeniably good *chef*, and that was the chief consideration. Gaëtan, this strange being informed us, was his name—speedily transformed by Gerôme into the more euphonious and romantic name of Gaetano!

I took leave of the Prince and my old friend the Wazir with some misgivings, for the new camel-drivers were Beïla men, and frankly owned that their knowledge of the country lying between Gwarjak and Noundra (where we were to leave the caravan-track) was derived chiefly from hearsay.

There are two caravan-roads through Beïla. One, formerly much used, is that over which we had travelled from the coast, and which, on leaving Beïla, leads due north to Quetta *viâ* Wadd and Sohrab. An ordinary caravan by this route occupies at least forty days in transit. Traffic is now, therefore, usually carried on by means of the safer trade-routes through British Sindh, whereby the saving of time is considerable, and chances of robbery much lessened. The second road (which has branches leading to the coast towns of Gwádar, Pasui, and Ormara) proceeds due west to Kej, capital of the Mekrán province, near the Persian border. The latter track we were to follow as far as Noundra, ninety miles distant. I should add that the so-called roads of Baluchistán are nothing more than narrow, beaten paths, as often as not entirely obliterated by swamp or brushwood. Beyond Noundra, where we left the main track to strike northwards for Gwarjak, there was absolutely nothing to guide us but occasional landmarks by day and the stars at night.

Barring the intense monotony, the journey was not altogether unenjoyable. To reach Noundra it took us five days. This may appear slow work, but quicker progress is next to impossible in a country where, even on the regular caravan-road, the guides are constantly losing the track, and two or three hours are often wasted in regaining it. The first two or three days of the journey lay through swampy ground, through which the camels made their way with difficulty, for a cat on the ice in walnut-shells is less awkward than a camel in mud. Broad deep swamps alternating with tracts of sandy desert, with nothing to relieve the monotonous landscape but occasional clumps of "feesh," a stunted palm about three feet in height, and rough cairns of rock erected by travellers to mark the pathway where it had become obliterated, sufficiently describes the scenery passed through for the first three days after leaving Beïla. Large stones accurately laid out in circles of eighteen or twenty feet in diameter were also met with at intervals of every two miles or so by the side of the track, and this very often in districts where nothing was visible but a boundless waste of loose, drifting sand. Our Baluchis could not or would not explain the *raison d'être* of them, though the stones must, in many instances, have been brought great distances and for a definite purpose. I could not, however, get any explanation regarding them at either Kelát or Quetta.

With the exception of the Lakh Pass leading over a chain of hills about eighteen miles due west of Beïla, the road to Noundra was as flat as a billiard-table. The crossing of the Lakh, however, was not accomplished without much difficulty and some danger; for the narrow pathway, leading over rocky, almost perpendicular, cliffs, three to four hundred feet high, had, in places, almost entirely crumbled away. The summits of these cliffs present a curious appearance—fifty to sixty needle-like spires, hardly a couple of feet thick at the top, which look as if the hand of man and not of nature had placed them in the symmetrical order in which they stand, white and clear-cut against the deep-blue sky, slender and fragile as sugar ornaments, and looking as though a puff of wind would send them toppling over. The ascent was terribly hard work for the camels, and, as the track is totally unprotected by guard-rail of any kind, anything but comfortable for their riders. Towards the summit we met a couple of these beasts laden with tobacco from Kej, in charge of a wild-looking fellow in rags, as black as a coal, who eyed us suspiciously, and answered in sulky monosyllables when asked where he hailed from. His merchandise, consisting of four small bags, seemed hardly worth the carrying, but Kej tobacco fetches high prices in Beïla. At this point the pathway had latterly been widened by order of the Djam. Formerly, if two camels travelling in opposite directions met, their respective owners drew lots. The animal belonging to the loser was then sacrificed and pushed over the precipice to clear the way for the other.

In the wet season a foaming torrent dashes through the Valley of Lakh, but this was, at the time of my visit, a dry bed of rock and shingle. Indeed, although we were fairly fortunate as regard wells, and I was never compelled to put the caravan on short allowance, I did not pass a single stream of running water the whole way from Sonmiani to Dhaïra, twenty miles south of Gwarjak, though we must in that distance have crossed at least fifteen dry river-beds, varying from twenty to eighty yards in width.

Travelling in the daytime soon became impossible, on account of the heat, as we proceeded further inland. A start was therefore generally made before it was light, and by 11 a.m. the day's work was over, tents pitched, camels turned loose, and a halt made till three or four the next morning. Though the sun at midday was, with the total absence of shade, dangerously powerful, and converted the interior of our canvas tents into the semblance of an oven, there was little to complain of as regards weather. The nights were deliciously cool, and the pleasantest part of the twenty-four hours was perhaps that from 8 till 10 a.m., when, dinner over and camp-fires lit, the Baluchis enlivened the caravan with song and dance. Baluch music is, though wild and mournful, pleasing. Some of the escort had fine voices, and sang to the accompaniment of a low, soft pipe, their favourite instrument. Gerôme was in great request on these occasions, and, under the influence of some fiery raki, of which he seemed to have an unlimited stock, would have trolled out "Matoushka Volga" and weird Cossack ditties till the stars were paling, if not suppressed. As it was, one got little enough rest, what with the heat and flies at midday, and, at the halt about 8 a.m., the shouting, hammering of tent-pegs, and braying of camels that went on till the sun was high in the heavens.

There is a so-called town or village, Jhow (situated about twenty miles east of Noundra), in a sparsely cultivated plain of the same name. Barley and wheat are grown by means of irrigation from the Jhow river, which in the wet season is of considerable size. I had expected to find, at Jhow, some semblance of a town or village, as the Wazir of Beïla had told me that the place contained a population of four or five hundred, and it is plainly marked on all Government maps. But I had yet to learn that a Baluch "town," or even village, of forty or fifty inhabitants often extends over a tract of country many miles in extent. The "town" of Jhow, for instance, is spread over a plain thirty-five miles long by fourteen broad, in little clusters of from two to six houses. A few tiny patches of green peeping out of the yellow sand and brushwood, a wreath of grey smoke rising lazily here and there at long intervals over the plain, a few camels and goats browsing in the dry, withered herbage by the caravan-track, showed that there were inhabitants; but we saw no dwellings, and only one native, a woman, who, at sight of Gerôme, who gallantly rode forward to address her, turned and fled as if she had seen the evil one. Noundra, which was reached on the 30th of March, was a mere repetition of Jhow. Neither houses nor natives were visible, though we passed occasional patches of cultivated ground. About five miles west of this we left the beaten track and struck out due north for Gwarjak, which, according to my calculation, lay about seventy miles distant.

CHAPTER X.

BALUCHISTÁN—GWARJAK.

Most European travellers through this desolate land have testified to the fact that the most commendable trait in the Baluch is his practice of hospitality, or "zang," as it is called. As among the Arabs, a guest is held sacred, save by some of the wilder tribes on the Afghan frontier, who, though they respect a stranger actually under their roof, will rob and murder him without scruple as soon as he has departed. The natives of Kanéro and Dhaïra (the two villages lying between Noundra and Gwarjak) were, though civil, evidently not best pleased at our appearance, but the sight of a well-armed escort prevented any open demonstration of ill feeling.

The first day's work after Noundra was rough, so much so that the camels could scarcely struggle through the deep sand, or surmount the steep, pathless ridges of slippery rock that barred our progress every two or three miles. Though the greater part of the journey lay through deep, drifting sand, the soil in places was hard and stony, and here the babul tree and feesh palm grew freely, also a pretty star-shaped yellow flower, called by Baluchis the "jour." This plant is poisonous to camels, but, strangely enough, harmless to sheep, goats, and other animals.

For a desert-journey, we had little to complain of as regards actual discomfort. There were no mosquitoes or sandflies, and the heat, though severe, was never excessive save for a couple of hours or so at midday, when enforced imprisonment in a thin canvas tent became rather trying. There was absolutely no shade—not a tree of any kind visible from the day we left Beïla till our arrival at Dhaïra about midday on the 31st of March. Scarcity of water was our greatest difficulty. At Noundra it had been salt and brackish; at Kanéro we searched in vain for a well. Had we known that a couple of days' march distant lay a land "with milk and honey blest," this would have inconvenienced us but little. The fact, however, that only three barrels of the precious liquid remained caused me some anxiety, especially as the first well upon which we could rely was at Gwarjak, nearly sixty miles distant.

The sight of Dhaïra, on the morning of the 31st, relieved us of all further anxiety. This fertile plain, about fifteen miles long by ten broad, is bounded on the north-west by a chain of limestone mountains, the name of which I was unable to ascertain. Here for the second time since Beïla we found a village and traces of inhabitants, the former encircled for a considerable distance by fields of maize and barley, enclosed by neat banks and hedges—a grateful contrast to the desolate waste behind us. It was the most perfect oasis imaginable. Shady forest trees and shrubs surrounded us on every side, a clear stream of running water fringed with ferns and wild flowers rippled through our camp, while the poor half-starved horses of the escort revelled in the long, rich grass. Hard by a cluster of three or four leaf huts, half hidden in a grove of date palms, lay (part of) the little village of Dhaïra, deserted at this busy hour of the day save by women and children. The latter fled upon our arrival, and did not reappear until the evening, when the return of the men reassured them sufficiently to approach our tents and look upon the strange and unwelcome features of the Farangi without fear.

From here, by advice of the Wazir of Beïla, a messenger was despatched to Malak, at Gwarjak, twenty miles distant, requesting permission to travel through his dominions. I resolved to proceed no further without the chief's sanction, or to afford him in any way an excuse for making himself unpleasant. In the mean time, arms and accoutrements were looked to, and the escort cleaned and smartened up as well as circumstances would permit. The natives overcame their shyness next morning, and brought us goat's milk and "rogan," or clarified butter. The Baluchis seldom eat meat, their food principally consisting of cakes or bread made of grain, with buttermilk and rice. A favourite preparation known as "shalansh," and called "krout" by the Afghans, is made by boiling buttermilk till the original quantity is reduced by half. The remainder is then strained through a thick felt bag, in the sun. When the draining ceases, the mass in the bag is formed into small lumps dried hard by the sun's rays. When required for use these lumps are pounded and placed in warm water, where they are worked by the hands until dissolved. The thickened fluid is then boiled with rogan and eaten with bread.

Assafoetida, indigenous to the country, is largely used among all classes for flavouring dishes. So much is this noxious plant liked by Baluchis, that it goes by the name of "khush-khorak," or pleasant food. At Kelát, in the palace of the Khan, I was offered it pickled, but it is usually eaten stewed in butter.

About midday, to my great surprise, Malak made his appearance in person, mounted on a good-looking chestnut stallion, its bridle and saddle adorned with gold and silver trappings. Four attendants followed on sorry-looking steeds. The chief, a tall, well-built fellow, about thirty years of age, with a sulky, sinister cast of countenance, was clad in a bright green satin jacket, white and gold turban, loose dark-blue trousers, and embroidered slippers. The loss of one eye gave him a still more unpleasant expression, a lock of coarse black hair being dragged over the face to conceal the disfigurement. The whole party were armed to the teeth, and carried guns, shields, and revolvers.

Our interview did not commence propitiously. Swinging himself off his horse, Malak returned my salutation with a sulky nod, and swaggered into the tent, signing to his suite to follow his example. Curtly refusing my offer of refreshment, he called for his pipe-bearer, and, lighting a kalyan, commenced puffing vigorously at some abominably smelling tobacco, which soon rendered the interior of the tent unbearable. It is, unfortunately, Baluch etiquette to allow a guest to open the conversation. Malak, well aware of this, maintained a stolid silence, and appeared hugely to enjoy the annoyance and impatience I tried in vain to conceal. It was not till nearly an hour had elapsed that this amiable visitor at last inquired, in a rude, surly tone, what I wanted. My interpreter's services were then called in, but it was not without demur and a long consultation with his suite that Malak consented to accompany me to Gwarjak on the morrow. Matters were finally arranged, on the understanding that I did not remain more than one day at Gwarjak, but proceeded to Kelát without delay.

I strolled out with a gun in the evening, and managed to bag a brace of partridges, which swarmed in the maize and barley fields. Overcoming the fears of the women, I was permitted to approach and inspect, though not enter, one of their dwellings. The latter, constructed of dried palm leaves, were about fifteen feet long by eight feet broad, and were entirely devoid of rugs, carpets, or furniture of any kind, and indescribably filthy. The men, though shy and suspicious, would have been friendly, had it not been for Malak, who followed me like a shadow; but nothing would induce the women and children to approach either Gerôme or myself. "What is this?" said one old fellow to Malak, stroking my face with his horny, grimy palm. "I never saw anything like it before." Most of the men were clothed in dirty, discoloured rags. The women wore simply a cloth tied loosely over the loins, while male and female children fourteen or fifteen years old ran about stark naked.

A curious flower, the "kosisant," grows luxuriantly about here. It is in shape something like a huge asparagus, and about two feet high, being covered from top to bottom with tiny white-and-yellow blossoms, with a sweet but sickly perfume. It consists but of one shoot or stalk, and bursts through the ground apparently with great force, displacing the soil for several inches.

We left for Gwarjak at 5.30 the following morning. Etiquette compelled Malak to offer me his horse, while he mounted my camel—an operation effected with very bad grace by my host. The Baluch saddle consists simply of two sharp pieces of wood bound together by leathern thongs, and the exchange was by no means a welcome one so far as I was concerned. Had it cut me in two, however, I would have borne it, if only to punish this boorish ruffian for his insolence of yesterday. Malak's chief failing was evidently vanity, and he was very reluctant, even for an hour, to cede the place of honour to a European.

The road for the first ten miles or so lay along the dry bed of a river, which, I ascertained with difficulty from my one-eyed companion, is named the Mashki. Large holes, from eight to ten feet deep, had been dug for some distance by the Dhaïra natives, forming natural cisterns or tanks. These were, even now, after a long spell of dry weather, more than half full, and the water, with which we filled barrels and flasks, clear, cold, and delicious.

The Shirengaz Pass, which crosses a chain of hills about five hundred feet high, separates the Dhaïra Valley from the equally fertile district of Gwarjak. The ascent and descent are gradual and easy, and by ten o'clock we were in sight of Gwarjak, before midday had encamped within half a mile of the town, if a collection of straggling tumble-down huts can so be called. The news of our arrival had preceded us, and before tents were pitched the population had turned out *en masse*, and a mob of quite two hundred men, women, and children were squatted around our camp, watching, at a respectful distance, the proceedings of my men with considerable interest. Malak had meanwhile disappeared, ostensibly to warn the Wazir of our arrival.

Gwarjak is situated on the left bank of the Mashki river, and consists of some thirty huts, shapeless and dilapidated, built of dried palm leaves. About two hundred yards north of the village rises a steep almost perpendicular rock about a hundred feet high, on the summit of which is perched a small mud fort. The latter is crenelated, loopholed for musketry, and mounts six cannon of a very primitive kind. It was at once apparent that we were anything but welcome. The very sight of my armed escort seemed to annoy and exasperate the male population, while the women and children gathered together some distance off, flying in a body whenever one of our party approached them. I looked forward, with some impatience, to Malak's return, for Kamoo's request for the loan of a knife from one of the bystanders was met with an indignant refusal, accompanied by murmuring and unmistakable expressions of hostility. We were well armed certainly, but were only ten men against over a hundred.

Our camping-place was wild and picturesque, and, had it not been for the uncomfortable sensation of not quite knowing what would happen next, our stay at Gwarjak would have been pleasant enough. Even Gerôme was depressed and anxious, and the Beïla men and escort ill at ease. I was sorely tempted more than once to accede to Kamoo's request, strike tents and move on to Gajjar, the next village, but was restrained by the thought that such a proceeding would not only be undignified, but a source of satisfaction to my *bête noire*, Malak.

After a prolonged absence of four or five hours, the latter returned, together with his Wazir and about a dozen followers. A more cut-throat looking set of ruffians I have seldom seen. All wore long black-cloth robes trimmed with scarlet, and white turbans, and carried a Snider rifle and belt stuffed with cartridges slung over the left shoulder. I now noticed with some anxiety that Malak's quiet and undemonstrative manner had completely altered to one of swaggering insolence and bravado. "The chief wishes you to know he has twenty more like this," said Kamoo, pointing to Malak's villainous-looking suite. "Tell him I am very glad to hear it," was my reply, politely meant, but which seemed to unduly exasperate the King of Gwarjak. Brushing past me, he burst into the tent, followed by his men, and seated himself on my only camp-stool. Then, producing a large American revolver, he cocked it with a loud click, placed it on the ground beside him, and called for his kalyan.

Patience has limits. With the reflection that few white men would have put up with the insults I had; that "Tommy Atkins" was, after all, only three hundred miles away; and that, in the event of my death, Malak would probably be shot, if not blown from a gun,—I ordered him (through the trembling Kamoo) to instantly leave the tent with all his followers. The fire-eating chieftain was (unlike most Baluchis) a poor creature, for to my intense relief he slunk out at once, with his tail between his legs. Having then re-appropriated the camp-stool, I ordered in the escort, fixed bayonets, loaded *my* revolver with ostentation, and commanded my friend to re-enter alone, which he did, and, as Americans say, "quickly."

MALAK

Then ensued an uncomfortable silence, interrupted by the arrival of one of my men to say that the villagers had refused to sell provisions of any kind, although eggs, milk, and rice were to be had in plenty. "I am not the king of these people," said Malak, passionately, on being remonstrated with. "Every man here is free to do as he pleases with his own." As our stores were now running uncomfortably short, this "Boycotting" system was anything but pleasant. "Will *you* sell us some eggs and milk?" I asked, as my unwilling guest rose to go. It was eating humble-pie with a vengeance, but hunger, like many other things, has no laws. "I am not a stall-keeper," was the answer. A request to be permitted to ascend the hill and visit the fort was met by an emphatic refusal. I then, as a last resource, inquired, through Kamoo, if my hospitable host had any objection to my walking through the village. "If you like," was the reply; "but I will not be responsible for your safety. This is not Kelát. The English are not our masters. We care nothing for them."

Notwithstanding these mysterious warnings, however, I visited the village towards sunset, alone with Gerôme, fearing lest the sight of my escort should arouse the ire and suspicions of the natives. There was little to see and nothing to interest. Gwarjak is built without any attempt at order or symmetry. Many of the houses had toppled over till their roofs touched the ground, and the whole place presented an appearance of poverty and decay strangely at variance with the smiling plains of grain, rice, and tobacco around it. Not a human being was visible, for our appearance was the signal for a general stampede indoors, but the dirty, narrow streets swarmed with huge, fierce dogs, who would have attacked us but for the heavy "nagaikas"[34] with which we were armed. We were evidently cordially hated by both men and beasts! On return to camp I gave orders for a start at four the next morning. There was no object to be gained by remaining, and the natives would have been only too glad of an excuse for open attack.

The remains of an ancient city, covering a very large area, are said to exist near Gwarjak, about a mile due south of it. I could, however, discover no trace of them, although we came from that direction, and must have traversed the supposed site.

After the fatigue and anxiety of the day, I was enjoying a cigar in the bright moonlight, when a messenger from the village arrived in camp. He had a narrow escape. Not answering the challenge of the sentry for the second time, the latter was about to fire, when I ran forward and threw up his rifle, which discharged in the air. A second later, and the man would have been shot, in which case I do not suppose we should ever have seen Quetta. The message was from Malak, inviting me to a "Zigri," a kind of religious dance, taking place just outside the village. After some reflection, I decided to go. It might, of course, mean treachery, but the probability was that the chief, afraid of being reported to the Indian Government for his insolence and insubordination, wished to atone for his conduct before I left.

Under the messenger's guidance, and attended by Gerôme and a guard of five men with loaded rifles, I set out. Both the Russian and myself carried and prominently displayed a brace of revolvers. A walk of ten minutes brought us to a cleared space by the river. In the centre blazed a huge bonfire, round which,

[34] Cossack whips.

in a semicircle, were squatted some two or three hundred natives, watching the twistings and contortions of half a dozen grotesque creatures with painted faces, and long, streaming hair, who, as they turned slowly round and round, varied the performance with leaps and bounds, alternately groaning, wailing, and screaming at the top of their voices.

A "ZIGRI" AT GWARJAK

A horn, a lute, and half a dozen tom-toms accompanied the dance. Some distance away, and surrounded by his grim-looking guard, sat Malak, who, though he did not rise to receive me, beckoned me to his side with more politeness than usual. It was a weird, strange sight. The repulsive, half-naked figures leaping round the fire, the silent, awestruck crowd of Baluchis, the wild barbaric music, and pillar of flame flashing on the dark, sullen face of Malak and his followers, was not a little impressive, especially as I was in a state of pleasing uncertainty as to the object of my host's sudden change of manner, and whether this might not be a little dramatic introduction to an attack upon our party. This was, however, evidently not my sulky friend's intention, for, as I rose to go, he actually stood up and took my hand. "At Gajjar," he said, "you will be able to get all you want, but take my advice, and get away from here early to-morrow morning. They do not like you."

Four hours after we were *en route*. The Zigri was still going on as we rode out of the village. Malak and his guard still sat motionless, the weird dancers and crowd of onlookers were still there, the huge bonfire blazing as brightly as ever, though the Eastern sky was lightening. As we passed within a hundred yards, I waved my hand, but the compliment was not returned. Some of the crowd looked up at the caravan; all must have seen it, but averted their faces till we had passed. I was not, on the whole, sorry to leave Gwarjak.

But one European, Colonel M—— of the Indian service, had visited Gwarjak for fifteen years prior to my visit. My road thither from Noundra has never been traversed save by natives, and it was, perhaps, more by good luck than good management that we came through successfully. The inhabitants of Gwarjak are a tribe known as the Nushirvanis, who claim to be of Persian descent. It was only at Quetta that I learnt that my friend Malak was only Viceroy of this inhospitable district. The head-quarters and residence of the Chief, one Nimrood Khan, is at Kharán (a hundred and fifty miles north-west of Gwarjak). Nimrood, who was fortunately absent, detests Europeans, and would probably have made matters even worse for us. Intermixed freely with the wild and lawless tribes of the Baluch-Afghan frontier (from which Kharán is but a few miles distant), it is scarcely to be wondered at that the Nushirvanis are inimical to Europeans, whom they are taught by their chiefs and Afghan neighbours to look upon as natural enemies.

Although we had not as yet formed a very favourable idea of Baluch hospitality, our reception at every village from here to the capital amply atoned for the rough and uncivil behaviour of the wild Nushirvanis. We were now once more on the beaten track, for though the country south of Gwarjak was, previous to our crossing it, unexplored, the journey from Kelát to Gajjar has frequently been made by Europeans during the past few years. Our reception by the natives of Gajjar (only twenty miles from Gwarjak) was a pleasant contrast to that given us at the latter place. Camp was no sooner pitched than presents of eggs, milk, rice, and tobacco were brought in, and I was cordially welcomed by the chief of the village.

Gajjar is a ramshackle, tumble-down place of about three hundred inhabitants. On a small hillock to the right of the village stands the fort, a square building of solid masonry, which, however, is now roofless, and has only three walls standing. The garrison (of six men) were lodged in a flimsy tent pitched in the centre of the ruins. Half the houses were constructed of dried mud; the remainder, as at Gwarjak, of palm leaves. The village stands in a grove of date palms, and the swarms of flies were consequently almost unendurable. We encamped close to the village well, to which, during the afternoon, many of the female population came to draw water. Two of them, bright, pleasant-featured girls of eighteen or twenty, were the best-looking specimens of the Baluch woman that I met with throughout the journey.

Towards sunset the corpse of a young man was borne past my tent and interred in a little cemetery hard by. The burial rites of the Baluchis are very similar to those of Persia. When a death occurs, mourners are sent for, and food is prepared at the deceased's house for such friends as desire to be present at the reading of prayers for the dead, while "kairats," or charitable distributions of food, are made for the benefit of the soul of the deceased. A wife, on the decease of her husband, neglects washing, and is supposed to sit lamenting by herself for not less than fifteen days. Long before this, however, her female friends come to her house and beg her to desist from weeping, bringing with them the powder of a plant called "larra." With this the widow washes her head, and then resumes her former life and occupations. If, however, by thoughtlessness or malice, her friends defer their visit, she must mourn for a much longer period alone. A curious Baluch custom is that of digging a grave much deeper for a woman than a man. They argue that woman is by nature so restless she would not remain quiet, even in death, without a larger proportion of earth over her.

NOMAD BALUCH TENT

In the matter of births and marriages the Baluchis, being of the Mohammedan religion, regulate their ceremonies mainly according to the Korán. Marriage is attended with great festivities. The first step is the "zang," or betrothal, which is regarded as of a very sacred nature, the final rite being known as "nikkar." On the wedding-day the bridegroom, gorgeously arrayed, and mounted on his best horse or camel, proceeds with his friends to a "ziarat," or shrine, there to implore a blessing, after which the "winnis," or marriage, is gone through by a moullah. On the birth of a child there is also much feasting. The fourth day after birth a name is given to the infant, and on the sixth an entertainment to friends. The following day the rite of circumcision ("kattam") is performed, though not always, this being sometimes postponed for a year or more. On this occasion (as at a death) large distributions of food are made to the poor.

The country between Gajjar and Jebri, which was reached next day, is bare and sterile, notwithstanding that, at the latter place, water is seldom scarce, even in the dryest seasons. The plain, which consists of loose, drifting sand, with intervals of hard, stony ground, is called Kandari. The cold here in the months of January and February is intense. We passed some curious cave-dwellings in the side of the caravan-track, in which the natives take refuge from the icy blasts that sweep across here in winter. They are formed by digging holes eight to ten feet deep. These are rudely thatched over with palm leaves, bits of stick, and plaited straw, thus forming a warm and comfortable shelter.

The Chief of Jebri, one Chabas Khan, rode out to meet me, clad in a long gown of golden thread, which, flashing in the sun, was discernible a couple of miles off. Jebri contains about four hundred inhabitants, and is a neatly built village, protected by a large mud fort, and a garrison of twenty Baluchis armed with Snider rifles. Chabas, who was very proud of his village, informed me that his rule extended over a considerable extent of country, containing a population of over 20,000. Many of his subjects were natives of Seistan, Kharán, and Shotrawák, all Afghan border districts, and gave him at times no little trouble. The Jebri fort had been attacked only a year previous to my visit, but Chabas (who I afterwards heard at Kelát is a renowned fire-eater) gave the rebels such a warm reception that there has been no outbreak since. My genial old host had himself given a good deal of trouble to the Kelát Government in his younger days, and told me with evident pride that he had led many a chupao in the good old days. The savage and predatory character of the Baluchi was formerly well exemplified in these lawless incursions, when large tracts of country were pillaged and devastated and the most unheard-of cruelties practised. Chupaos are now a thing of the past. Pottinger, who traversed this country in the last century, and had more than one unpleasant *rencontre* with these armed bands, thus describes one of these plundering expeditions—

"The depredators are usually mounted on camels, and furnished, according to the distance they have to go, with food, consisting of dates, goat's milk, and cheese. They also carry water in a small skin-bag, if requisite, which is often the case if the expedition is prolonged. When all is prepared the band sets off and marches incessantly till within a few miles of where the chupao is to commence, and then halts in some unfrequented spot to rest their camels. On the approach of night they mount again, and, as soon as the inhabitants of a village have retired to rest, begin their attack by burning, destroying, and carrying off whatever comes in their way. They never think of resting for one moment during the chupao, but ride on over the territory on which it is made at the rate of eighty or ninety miles a day, until they have loaded their camels with as much pillage as they can possibly remove; and as they are very expert in the management of their animals, each man on an average will have charge of ten or twelve. If practicable, they make a circuit which enables them to return by a different route. This affords a double prospect of plunder and also misleads those who pursue the robbers—a step generally taken, though with little effect, when a sufficient body of men can be collected for that purpose."

"In these desperate undertakings the predatory robbers are not always successful, and when any of them chance to fall into the hands of exasperated villagers, they are mutilated and put mercilessly to death. The fact," concludes Pottinger, "of these plundering expeditions being an institution in Baluchistán must serve to show how slight is the power wielded by the paramount rulers, and what risks to the safety of both person and property must be run by those engaged in the business of trade in such a country."

Chabas visited me towards evening, accompanied by his son, a clever-looking, bright-eyed lad about fifteen years old. Noticing that he wore a belt and buckle of the 66th Regiment, I inquired where he had procured it, and was told that it had been purchased from a Gwarjak man, who brought it down from Kharán shortly after the fatal disaster to the regiment at Maiwand. The kindly old chief now pressed my acceptance of a fine fat goat—a very acceptable gift, considering the impoverished condition of the camp larder. We then visited the fort and village, under his guidance.

Jebri and its neighbourhood are well cultivated. The system of agriculture practised in this part of Baluchistán is simple, but effective, the fields being divided off by ridges of earth and raised embankments to an accurate level. They are then further subdivided longitudinally by ridges thrown up about seven or eight paces apart. This is done for purposes of irrigation. The soil is then ploughed and manured, the former operation being generally carried on by means of bullocks. Tracts of land not irrigated by streams, but which are dependent on rain and the rivulets which come down from the hillsides after it, are called "kash-kawa," and are found scattered about the valleys here and there near the tent-encampments of the nomad tribes, who plough a piece of land, sow it, and return to gather in the crop when it is matured. The implements of husbandry in general use are a light wooden plough of primitive construction, consisting of a vertical piece bent forward at the bottom and tipped with an iron point, and a long horizontal beam, which passes forward between the pair of bullocks that draw it, and is fastened to the yoke. A harrow, consisting of a wooden board about six feet long by two wide, is also used, being dragged over the ploughed land attached to the yoke by iron chains. If found not sufficiently heavy, the driver stands upon it. A spade or shovel, exactly like its English counterpart, and a reaping-hook, or sickle, having its cutting edge furnished with minute teeth, complete the list of a Baluchi's agricultural tools.

JEBRI

Jebri Fort stands on a steep hillock about fifty feet in height. From here a good view was obtainable of the surrounding country. Immediately below were pretty gardens or enclosed spaces, sown in the centre with maize, wheat, and tobacco, and surrounded by plum and pomegranate trees and date palms. There is a considerable trade in the latter between here and Beïla, which perhaps accounted for the myriads of flies which here, as at Gajjar, proved a source of great annoyance. In Chabas's garden were roses and other flowers, some remarkably fine vines, and a number of mulberry trees. The grounds were well and neatly laid out with paths, grass plots, and artificial streams, upon which I complimented the old man; but he would talk of nothing but his fort, which was, indeed, the only structure worthy of the name met with between Quetta and the sea. In the evening his son brought me a delicious dish of preserved apricots and cream, for which I presented him with three rupees, one of which he instantly returned. It is considered, by Baluchis, extremely unlucky to give or accept an odd number of coins.

At Jebri, for the first time, we suffered severely from cold at night, the thermometer dropping to 42° Fahr. just before sunrise. The climate of Baluchistán presents extraordinary varieties, and is extremely trying to Europeans. Although at Kelát the natives suffer considerably more from cold in winter than summer heats, the hot season in the low-lying valleys and on the coast, which lasts from April till October, may be almost said to be the most severe in the world. At Kej, in Mekram, the thermometer sometimes registers 125° Fahr. in the shade as early as April, while the heat in the same district during the "Khurma-Paz," or "Date-ripening," is so intense that the natives themselves dare not venture abroad in the daytime.

Notwithstanding this, even the south of Baluchistán has its cold season. Near Beïla, in the month of January, the temperature frequently falls as low as 35° Fahr. in the mornings, rising no higher than 65° at any portion of the day. At Kelát, on the other hand, which stands 6800 feet above sea-level, the extreme maximum heat as yet recorded during the months of July and August is only 103° Fahr., while the extreme minimum during the same months is as low as 48° Fahr. In winter the cold is intense. Pottinger, the traveller, relates that on the 7th of February, 1810, when at Baghivana, five marches from Kelát, his water-skins were frozen into masses of ice, and seven days afterwards, at Kelát, he found the frost so intense that water froze instantly when thrown upon the ground. Bellew, a more recent traveller, in the month of January found the temperature even lower, as when at Rodinjo, thirteen miles south of Kelát, the thermometer at 7 a.m. stood at 14° Fahr., while the next night, at Kelát, it fell to 8° Fahr. The weather was at the time clear, sharp, and cold, the ground frozen hard all day, while snow-wreaths lay in the shelter of the walls. A detailed account of the eight days' journey from Gajjar to Kelát would weary the reader. A description of one village will suffice for all, while the country between these two places is nothing but bare, stony desert, varied by occasional ranges of low rocky hills, and considerable tracts of cultivated land surrounding the villages of Gidar, Sohrab, and Rodingo, at each of which we were well received by the natives. With the exception of a strike among our camel-drivers, which fortunately lasted only a few hours, and a dust-storm encountered a few miles from

Sohrab, nothing worthy of mention occurred to break the monotony of the voyage till, on the morning of the *9th of* April, we sighted the flat-roofed houses, mud ramparts, and towering citadel of the capital of Baluchistán.

CHAPTER XI.

KELÁT—QUETTA—BOMBAY.

We encamped in the suburbs of the city, about a couple of miles from the northern or Mastung Gate, and near the telegraph office, a small brick bungalow in charge of an English-speaking native. There is a single wire laid to Quetta, a distance, roughly speaking, of ninety miles. A terrific hurricane, accompanied by thunder, vivid lightning, and dense clouds of black dust, sprang up about sunset the day of our arrival. Both tents were instantly blown down, and in a few moments reduced to shapeless rags of torn canvas. So great was the force of the wind that it snapped the tent-poles short off, and, tearing them from the ropes, sent the tents flying over the plain as if they had been shreds of tissue paper. We managed, however, to find quarters in the telegraph office, and remained there till our departure, two days later, for Quetta. During the storm the thermometer sank to 50° Fahr., although a few moments before it had marked 78°.

Kelát contains—with its suburbs, which are of considerable extent—about 15,000 inhabitants, and is picturesquely situated on the edge of a fertile plain thickly cultivated with wheat, barley, and tobacco. The city is built in terraces, on the sides and summit of a limestone cliff, about a hundred and fifty feet high. This is called the "Shah Mirdan," and is surrounded at the base of the hill by high mud ramparts, with bastions at intervals, loopholed for musketry. The "Mir,"[35] or palace of the Khan, overhangs the town, and is made up of a confused mass of buildings, which, though imposing at a distance, I found on closer inspection to consist chiefly of mud, which in many places had crumbled away, leaving great gaping holes in the walls. The Mir mounts a few primitive, muzzle-loading cannon, and the citadel is garrisoned by a thousand men, chiefly Afghans, deserters from Cábul, Kandahár, and other parts of the Ameer's dominions. They are a ragged, undisciplined lot. The Khan himself has a wholesome dread of his soldiery, who break out at times, and commit great depredations among the villages surrounding the capital, robbing and murdering the peasants with impunity, for few dare resist them. The remainder of the troops, three thousand in number, are quartered in barracks, or rather mud hovels, at some distance from the palace. Each man is supposed to receive three rupees a month and a lump sum of forty-eight rupees at the end of each year, but pay is uncertain and mutiny frequent. When not engaged on military duties the Khan's Baluch soldiers are put to agricultural work on his estates, while the Afghans pass their time in pillaging and plundering their neigh-

[35] Parts of this palace are of great antiquity, as it owes its foundation to the Hindu kings who preceded the Mohammedan dynasty.

bours. As we entered Kelát we passed a regiment at drill on a sandy plain outside the walls. With the exception of a conical fur cap, there is no attempt at uniform. The men, fine strapping fellows, are armed with rusty flint-locks. Though there appeared to be no officers, European or otherwise, I was rather surprised to hear the word of command given in English, and to see this band of ragamuffins march off parade to the strains of "Home, sweet Home," played by a very fair fife-and-drum band.

The morning following my arrival, I was startled by the apparition at my bed-side of a swarthy, wild-looking Afghan sowar—a messenger from the Wazir, to say that his Highness the Khan wished to make my acquaintance, and would receive me, if convenient, at three o'clock that afternoon. It had not been my intention to solicit an interview, for, from all accounts, the Khan is anything but friendly towards Europeans, Englishmen in particular. To refuse, however, was out of the question. The morning was therefore devoted to cleaning up, and getting out a decent suit of wearing-apparel; while my Beïla escort, who evidently had uncomfortable forebodings as to the appearance of the Beïla uniform in the streets of Kelát, polished up arms and accoutrements till they shone like silver, and paid, I noticed, particular attention to the loading of their rifles and revolvers.

About midday the Wazir made his appearance to conduct me to the palace. He was a fat, paunchy old man, with beady black eyes and a shy, shifty expression, very unlike my cheery little friend at Beïla. After the usual preliminary questions as to who I was, my age, business, etc., he anxiously inquired after the health of Mr. Gladstone, and somewhat astonished me by asking whether I was a Liberal or Conservative. "You have some Beïla men with you, I see," said the Khan's adviser, who spoke English perfectly. "Don't let his Highness see them." I could not, after such a speech, allow my faithful escort to enter the city without warning. But it had little effect. "Let the dogs do what they like," was the reply. "We shall not let the sahib go alone."

Tea and cigarettes discussed, a start was made for the palace. The Wazir, on a wiry, good-looking bay horse, and attended by half a dozen mounted Afghans, led the way, and I followed on a pony borrowed of the telegraph clerk. My costume was, if not becoming, at any rate original: high boots, flannel trousers, and shirt, an evening dress-coat, and astrakhan cap. Gerôme's wardrobe being even less presentable, I deemed it prudent to leave him behind. The Beïla men brought up the rear of the procession some distance from the Afghans, who, to my anxiety, never ceased scoffing and jeering at them the whole way. Every moment I expected to hear the crack of a pistol-shot, followed by a general *mêlée*. Arrived at the Mastung Gate, we dismounted, and, leaving our horses in charge of the guard, slowly proceeded up the steep narrow streets to the citadel.

The entrance to Kelát is not imposing. There had been a good deal of rain, and the streets of the lower part of the town were perfect quagmires of mud nearly knee-deep. It was more like crawling into a dark passage than entering a city. Many of the thoroughfares are entirely covered over with wooden beams plastered with mud, which entirely exclude light, and give them more the appearance of subterranean passages than streets. The upper part of the town is the cleanest, for the simple reason that all filth and sewage runs down open gutters cut in the centre of the steep alleys, until it reaches the level of the plain. There is no provision made for its escape. It is allowed to collect in great pools, which in long-continued wet weather often flood the houses and drive their wretched inhabitants into the open, to live as best they may, further up the hill.

Kelát is, for this reason only, very unhealthy. Smallpox, typhoid, and typhus are never absent, though, curiously enough, cholera visitations are rare. The filthy habits of the inhabitants have, apparently, a good deal to do with the high death rate. I saw, while walking up the hill, a native fill a cup from an open drain and drink it off, although the smell was unbearable, the liquid of a dark-brown colour. A very common and—in the absence of medical treatment—fatal disease among the inhabitants of the suburbs (chiefly Afghans) is stone in the bladder, the water here, though pure and clear in the suburbs, containing a large quantity of lime.

The bazaar, through which we passed on our way to the Mir, does not seem a very busy one. Although not a public or religious holiday, many of the stalls were closed. Kelát was once the great channel for merchandise from Kandahár and Cábul to India, but the caravan trade is now insignificant. There is in the season a considerable traffic in dates, but that is all, for the roads to Persia and Afghanistán are very unsafe. Only a few weeks previous to my visit, a Kelát merchant, proceeding with a large caravan to Kermán, in Persia, was robbed and murdered in the frontier district west of Kharán. Few now attempt the journey, most of the goods being sent to Quetta, and thence by rail to various parts of India, by sea to Persia.

Art and industry are, as well as trade, practically at a standstill in the Khan's city, though a handsome embroidery, peculiar to Kelát, is made by the women, and fetches high prices in India, while some of the natives are clever at brass work and ironmongery. Noticing a Russian samovar in one of the shops, I entered and inquired of the owner (through the Wazir) how it had reached Kelát. "From Russia," was the reply, "*viâ* Meshéd, Herat, and Kandahár. There is a good caravan-road the whole way," added the Baluchi, taking down a small brass shield from a peg in the wall. "This came from Bokhára, *viâ* Cábul, only ten days ago; but trade is not what it was." "Would there be any difficulty in making that journey?" I asked. "For you—an Englishman—yes," said the man, with a queer smile, and was continuing, when "The Khan will be growing impatient," broke in the Wazir, taking my hand and leading me hurriedly into the street.

An Afghan guard of honour was drawn up at the entrance of the palace, wearing the nearest approach to a uniform I had yet seen—dark-green tunics, light-blue trousers, and white turbans, clean, well fitting, and evidently kept for state occasions. Each man carried a Berdán rifle and cavalry sabre. It struck me as a curious coincidence that the former rifle is in general use throughout the Russian army. Leaving my escort with strict injunctions to keep their tempers, and under no circumstances to allow themselves to be drawn into a quarrel, I followed the Wazir and his attendants into the Mir. The entrance is through an underground passage about forty yards long by seven wide, ill-smelling and in total darkness. Arrived at the end, we again emerged into daylight, and, ascending a flight of rickety wooden steps, found ourselves in the durbar-room—a spacious apartment, its walls decorated with green, gold, and crimson panels, alternating with large looking-glasses. Costly rugs and carpets from Persia and Bokhára strewed the grimy floor of the chamber, which is about sixty feet long, and commands a splendid view of the city and fertile plains beyond. Awaiting me upon the balcony was the Khan, surrounded by his suite and another guard of Afghans. A couple of dilapidated cane-bottomed chairs were then brought and set one on each side of the crimson velvet divan occupied by his Highness. Having made my bow, which was acknowledged by a curt nod, I was conducted to the seat on the right hand of the Khan by Azim Khan, his son, who seated himself upon his father's left hand. The Wazir, suite, soldiers, and attendants then squatted round us in a semicircle, and the interview commenced.

A long silence followed, broken only by the whish of the fly-brush as a white-clad Baluchi whisked it lazily to and fro over the Khan's head. The balcony on which we were received is poised at a dizzy height over the beehive-looking dwellings and narrow, tortuous streets of the brown city, which to-day were bathed in sunshine. The Khan's residence is well chosen. The pestilent stenches of his capital cannot ascend to this height, only the sweet scent of hay and clover-fields, and the distant murmur of a large population, while a glorious panorama of emerald-green plain stretches away to a rocky, picturesque range of hills on the horizon.

His Highness Mir Khudadad, Khan of Kelát, is about sixty years old. He would be tall were it not for a decided stoop, which, together with a toothless lower jaw, gives him the appearance of being considerably more than his age. His complexion is very dark, even for a Baluch, and he wears a rusty black beard and moustaches, presumably dyed, from the streaks of red and white that run through them, and long, coarse pepper-and-salt locks streaming far below his shoulders. His personal appearance gave me anything but a favourable impression. The Khan has a scowling expression, keen, piercing black eyes, and a sharp hooked nose that reminded one forcibly of Cruikshank's picture of Fagin the Jew in "Oliver Twist."

The Khan was dressed in a long, loose, white garment, with red silk embroidery of beautiful workmanship. A thin white Cashmere shawl was thrown carelessly over his shoulders, and he wore a conical violet silk cap, trimmed with gold lace, and a pair of pointed green morocco slippers, turned up at the toes, and ornamented with the same material. A massive gold necklace, or collar, thickly studded with diamonds, rubies, and sapphires, hung round his neck. The stones, some of them of great size, were set indiscriminately without any regard to pattern or design. Mir Khudadad wore no other jewels, with the exception of three small torquoise rings, all worn on the little finger of the left hand. He carried no arms, but held in his right hand a large and very dirty pocket-handkerchief of a bright yellow hue with large red spots, which somewhat detracted from his regal appearance. The Khan is a great snuff-taker, and during the audience continually refreshed himself from the contents of a small gold box carried by his son. Prince Azim, who was dressed in a green silk jacket and loose magenta-coloured trousers, is a pleasant-mannered lad of about twenty. He is of much lighter complexion than his father and has a strong Jewish cast of feature. A huge cabochon emerald of great value, suspended from the neck, was Azim's sole ornament.

KELÁT

A conversation now commenced, carried on through the medium of the Wazir and my interpreter. The Khan has a fidgety, uneasy manner that must be intensely exasperating to his court. More than once during the audience, having asked a question with much apparent earnestness, he would suddenly break in, in the middle of a reply, and hum a tune, or start off on a totally different subject from the one under discussion. At other times he would repeat a question twice or thrice, and, his eyes fixed on vacancy, utterly ignore the answers of the Wazir, who evidently stood in great awe of his eccentric sovereign. Though the following colloquy may appear brief to the reader, it took nearly an hour to get through.

"Where do you come from, and what are you?" was the Khan's first question.

"From Russia, your Highness."

"From Russia!" returned the Khan, quickly. "But you are English, are you not?"

"Certainly I am."

"How strong is Russia's army?" continued the Khan, after an application to the gold snuff box, and a trumpet-blast on the yellow bandanna.

"Nominally about three millions."

"And England?"

"About two hundred thousand, not counting the reserves."

"Humph!" grunted the Khan. "Tell me, do the English imagine that Abdur Raman[36] is their friend?"

"I believe so."

"Then tell them from me," cried the Khan, excitedly, half rising from his seat, "tell Queen Victoria from me that it is not so. Tell her to beware of Abdur Raman. He is her enemy."

"Is England afraid of Russia?" continued the Khan after a long pause.

"No; the English fear no one."

"Will England reach Kandahár before Russia takes Herat?"

"I really cannot say," was my answer to this somewhat puzzling question.

Mir Khudadad then turned away to converse with the Wazir in a low tone. About ten minutes elapsed, during which a long confabulation was held, in which many of the suite, including the Afghan soldiers, joined. Prince Azim meanwhile invited me to inspect his sword and pistols. The former, a splendid Damascus blade, and hilt encrusted with jewels, I especially admired. Had I known the use to which it had been put that morning, I should not, perhaps, have been so enthusiastic.

Again the Khan addressed me.

"Do you know Russia well?"

---

[36] The Ameer of Afghanistán.

PALACE OF H.H. THE KHAN, KELÁT

"Pretty well."

"Is it true that the Russians do not allow Mohammedans to worship in Central Asia?"

"I believe that is untrue."

"It is a lie?"

"Most certainly it is."

"Your own countrymen told me so." At this there was a roar of laughter, in which the Khan joined.

The durbar-room of Kelát reminded me of an English court of justice. When the Khan laughed his courtiers did, and *vice versâ*. After an interval of more snuff-taking and whispering, the Khan drew forth and examined my watch. Taking this for a polite hint that the interview had lasted long enough, I rose to go, but was at once thrust back into my chair by Azim. "You are not to go," said the Wazir. "The Khan is much interested by you."

"Dhuleep Singh is in Russia, is he not?" then asked the Khan.

"Yes."

"What does Russia pay him a year?"

"I do not know."

"More than England did?"

"I do not know."

"You English never do know anything," muttered the Khan, impatiently; adding, "Do you know the Czar of Russia?"

"I have seen him."

"Is he a good man?"

"I believe him to be so."

"Then why do his people try to kill him?"

"Some of them are Socialists."

"Socialists!" repeated the Khan, slowly. "What is that?"

I then explained with some difficulty the meaning of the word.

"Humph!" was the rejoinder. Then, with a whisk of the yellow bandanna: "I am glad I have none in Kelát!"

A mark of great favour was then shown me, the Khan presenting me with his photograph, with the request that I would show it to "Parliament" when I got home. I think he was under the impression that the latter is a human being. An incident that occurred but two years since is typical of the intelligence of the ruler of Kelát and his court. It was at Quetta, on the occasion of the presentation of Mir Khudadad to the Viceroy of India. Previous to a grand *déjeûner* given in his honour, the Khan and his suite were shown into a dressing-room for the purpose of washing their hands. On entering to announce that luncheon was ready, the aide-de-camp found that the distinguished guests had already commenced operations, and were greedily devouring the cakes of Pears' soap that had been placed there for a somewhat different purpose. That none of the party felt any after ill effects speaks well for the purity of the wares of the mammoth advertiser—or the Baluch digestion!

THE KHAN OF KELÁT

The Khan shook my hand cordially at parting, and again begged me not to forget his warnings anent the Ameer of Afghanistán, with whom he is apparently not on the best of terms. I found, with some relief, that my Beïla men had made friends with the Afghans, and, surrounded by an admiring crowd, were hobnobbing over a hissing samovar. One of the Afghans handed me a glass of tea, which, not to offend him, I drank and found delicious. It had come from China *viâ* Siberia, Samarcand, and Cábul. "Russki!" said the man with a grin, as I handed back the cup.

The Khan of Kelát very rarely leaves his palace, and is seldom seen abroad in the streets of Kelát except on Fridays, when he goes to the mosque on foot, attended by an escort armed to the teeth. He is said to live in constant dread of assassination, for his cruel, rapacious character has made him universally detested in and around the capital. His one thought in life is money and the increase of his income, which, with the yearly sum allowed him by the British Government, may be put down at considerably over £30,000 per annum. A thorough miser, the Khan does not, like most Eastern potentates, pass the hours of night surrounded by the beauties of the harem, but securely locked in with his money-bags in a small, comfortless room on the roof of his palace.

There is not the smallest doubt in my mind that Russian influence is, indirectly, being brought to bear on the Court of Kelát. But Mir Khudadad may be said to have no policy. As the French say, "Il change sa nationalité comme je change de chemise," and is to be bought by the highest bidder.

Although the Khan's subjects are heavily taxed, there is no protection whatsoever of life or property in or around Kelát. Theft is, according to the penal code, punished by fine and imprisonment, murder and adultery by death; but the law is subject to great modifications. In a word, the Khan is the law, and so long as a man can afford to pay or bribe him handsomely, he may commit the most heinous offences with impunity.

Two instances of the way in which justice is carried out happened just before I arrived at Kelát. In the one, a young Baluch woman was found by her husband, a soldier, under circumstances which admitted no doubt of her infidelity. Upon discovery, which took place at night, the infuriated husband rushed off to the guard-house for his weapon. During his absence the woman urged her lover, who was well armed, to meet and slay him in the darkness. Under pretence of so doing the gay Lothario left his paramour, but, fearful of consequences, made off to Quetta.

On his return home the husband used no violence, simply handing his wife over to the guard to be dealt with according to law. Brought before the Khan the next day, she was lucky enough to find that monarch in a good temper. Her beauty probably obtained the free pardon accorded her, and an order that her husband was also to condone her offence. The latter said not a word, took her quietly home in the evening, and cut her throat from ear to ear. The Khan, on hearing of the murder next day, made no remonstrance, nor was the offender punished. He was an Afghan.

The second case is even more disgraceful. One of the Khan's own suite, a well-known libertine and drunkard, contracted an alliance with a young girl of eighteen. He had endeavoured in vain to marry her younger sister, almost a child, and so beautiful that she was known for many miles round the city as the "Pearl of Kelát."

Six weeks after marriage this ruffian, in a fit of drunken frenzy caused by jealousy, almost decapitated his wife with a tulwar, and afterwards mutilated her body past recognition. The shrieks of the poor woman having summoned the neighbours, he was seized, bound, and led before the Khan, who at once sentenced him to death. The execution was fixed for sunrise the following day. At midnight, however, a messenger appeared at the gates of the Mir with a canvas bag containing two thousand rupees. "Tell him he is free," said the ruler of Kelát. "And if he sends in another thousand, I will *order* the younger sister to marry him." The money was paid, and the poor child handed over to the tender mercies of the human devil who had so ruthlessly butchered her sister.

I have mentioned that Azim Khan showed me a sword of beautiful workmanship. It had, the very morning of my visit to the palace, cut down and hacked to pieces a waiting-maid, not sixteen years old, in the Khan's harem. I myself saw the corpse of the poor girl the same evening, as it was being carried outside the walls for interment.[37]

This, then, is the state of things existing at Kelát, not a hundred miles from the British outposts; this the enlightened sovereign who has been made "Companion of the Star of India," an order which, among his own people, he affects to look upon with the greatest contempt.

The few women I saw at Kelát were distinctly good looking, far more so than those further south. Most of them have an Italian type of face, olive complexion, and large dark eyes, with sweeping lashes. But very few wore the hideous nose-rings so common at Beïla and Sonmiani. Morality is at a discount in the capital, and prostitution common.

The Wazir sent me a bag of dates the morning of my departure, with a short note, written in English, begging that I would send him in return the best gold watch and rifle "that could be bought for gold" in London. The note ended jocosely, "Exchange is no robbery!" The old man seemed well *au fait* with Central Asian affairs. On my mentioning the day before that I had intended entering India *viâ* Cábul, he at once said, "Ah! I supposed Alikhanoff stopped you. He is very shy of strangers."

We left Kelát at 6 a.m. on the 12th of April. The camels and heavy baggage had been sent on four or five hours previously to Mangachar, the first station. Our caravan now consisted of only eight camels, which we found reduced to seven on arrival. Just before daylight a couple of panthers had appeared close to the caravan and caused a regular stampede, the beasts flying right and left. On order being restored, two were found to be missing, one laden with the only small remaining tent and some native luggage, the other with a couple of cases of whisky (nearly empty) and my camp-stool. The former was traced and brought in after a search of over two hours, but the latter is still, for aught I know, careering over the boundless desert, an unconscious advertiser of "Jameson and Co." I afterwards heard that this plain is noted for panther and wolf, also an animal called the "peshkori," somewhat larger than a cat, with a reddish-coloured hide. It moves about the country in packs, carrying off deer and sheep. Its method of descending precipices and steep hillsides is curious, each animal fixing its teeth in the tail of another, thus

[37] I am not at liberty to give the name of my authority for these facts. The reader may rely on their authenticity.

forming a kind of chain.

The plain of Mangachar is situated nearly 6000 feet above sea-level, and is well cultivated with wheat, lucerne, and tobacco. The village itself is neatly laid out, and contains about three hundred inhabitants. The different aspects of the country north and south of Kelát are striking. We had now done with deserts for good, for at night lights were seen twinkling all over the plain, while in the daytime large tracts of well-cultivated land continually met the eye.

Between Mangachar and Mastung a hot wind arose, which made the eyes smart, and dried up the skin like a blast from a furnace. One's hair felt as it does in the hottest room of a Turkish bath, with the unpleasant addition of being filled with fine gritty sand. "I hope this may not end in a juloh," said Kamoo, anxiously. This, my interpreter proceeded to explain, is a hot poisonous wind peculiar to these districts, and perhaps the greatest danger run by travellers in Baluchistán. The warm breeze, as Kamoo called it, that we experienced was, though almost unbearable, not dangerous, while the dreaded juloh has slain its hundreds of victims. Cook, the traveller, who has given this subject much attention, has come to the conclusion that it is caused by the generation in the atmosphere of a highly concentrated form of ozone, by some intensely marked electrical condition. As evidence of its effect in destroying every green thing on its course, and in being frequently fatal to human life, he cites the following well-authenticated cases, which, not having encountered the death-dealing blast myself, I place before the reader:—

(1) In the year 1851, during one of the hot months, certain officers of the Sind Horse were sleeping at night on the roof of General Jacob's house at Jacobabad. They were awakened by a sensation of suffocation and an exceedingly hot and oppressive feeling in the air, while at the same time a very powerful smell of sulphur was noticed. On the following morning a number of trees in the garden were found to be withered in a very remarkable manner. It looked as if a current of fire, about two yards in breadth, had passed through the garden in a perfectly straight line, singeing and destroying every green thing in its course. Entering on one side, and passing out at the other, its tract was as clearly defined as the course of a river.

(2) At the close of 1856 a party of five men were crossing the desert of Shikarpur, being on their way from Kandahár to that city, when the blast crossed their path, killing three of them instantly and seriously disabling the other two.

(3) A "moonshi" with two companions was travelling about seven miles south-east of Bagh, in Kachi (not far distant from Mangachar). About two o'clock the blast struck them. They were sensible of a scorching sensation in the air, accompanied by a peculiar sulphurous smell, but remembered nothing further, as all three were immediately struck to the ground. They were afterwards found and carried to Bagh, where, every attention being afforded them, they ultimately, after many days of sickness, recovered.

As regards the strength of the juloh, Pottinger writes that, so searching is its nature, it has been known to kill camels and other hardy animals, and its effects on the human frame are said by eye-witnesses to be the most agonizing and repulsive imaginable. Shortly after contact with the wind the muscles of the sufferer become rigid and contracted, the skin shrivels, a terrible sensation as if the skin were on fire pervades the whole frame, while, in the last stage, the skin cracks into deep gashes, producing haemorrhage, quickly followed by death. It is curious to note that the juloh is peculiar to the northern districts of Sarawán and Kach-Gandáva, and does not exist in the southern provinces of Baluchistán.

The road from Mangachar to Mastung is good, though slightly undulating, and intersected by deep "nullahs." The estimated area of the Mastung district is two hundred and eighty miles. It is aptly named "The Garden of Baluchistán," for considerably more than two-thirds of its area are under cultivation. Water at Mastung is never-failing, and the pretty town, nestling in a valley of vineyards and fruit-gardens, fig and olive trees, reminded one more of some secluded town in the Pyrenees or south of France than a Baluch settlement. The soil hereabouts is light and sandy and particularly favourable to the cultivation of grapes, of which there are no less than five kinds. Apricots, peaches, plums, and pomegranates are also grown, and supply the markets of Quetta and Kelát. Madder and tobacco are also exported in large quantities from Mastung, which possesses a neatly built and busy bazaar.

The plain of Dasht-bi-Dowlat, or "The Unpropitious Plain," lies between Mastung and Quetta. The name, however, only applies after the harvest has been gathered, for next to Mastung this is one of the most fertile spots in Baluchistán. Dasht-bi-Dowlat is mainly cultivated by wandering tribes. The inhabitants of Mastung were enthusiastic in their description of the plain in summer. Then, they told us, the surface is covered with verdure and flowers of all kinds, especially the "lala," or tulip, which they averred cover it for miles with a carpet of crimson and gold, and load the air with sweet intoxicating perfume. The cultivation of this plain is mostly dependent on rain and heavy dews.

To the west of Dasht-bi-Dowlat is Chehel-Tan, a steep, rocky mountain, 13,000 feet high, in the ravines and valleys of which snow still lay deeply. Only two Europeans, Masson the traveller, and Sir Henry Green, have ever succeeded in reaching the summit, on which is a "Zariat," or shrine. The ascent is difficult and dangerous, as, the mountain being said to be haunted, no native guides are procurable. The word "Chehel-Tan" signifies in Baluch "Forty Bodies," and is derived from the following legend.

A frugal pair, many years married, were unblest with offspring. They therefore sought the advice of a holy man, who rebuked the wife, saying that he had not the power to grant her what Heaven had denied. The priest's son, however (also a moullah), felt convinced he could satisfy her wishes, and cast forty pebbles into her lap, at the same time praying that she might bear children. In process of time she was delivered of forty babes—rather more than she wished or knew how to provide for. The poor husband, at his wits' end, ascended to the summit of Chehel-Tan with thirty-nine, and left them there, trusting to the mercy of the Deity to provide for them, while the fortieth babe was brought up under the paternal roof.

One day, however, touched by remorse, the wife, unknown to her husband, explored the mountain with the object of collecting the bones of her children and burying them. To her surprise, they were all living and gambolling among the trees and rocks. Wild with joy, she ran back to her dwelling, brought out the fortieth babe, and, placing it on the summit of the mountain, left it there for a night to allure back its brothers, but, on returning in the morning, she found that the latter had carried it off, and it was never seen again. It is by the spirits of these forty babes that Chehel-Tan is said to be haunted.

At 8 a.m. on the 14th of April we sighted, afar off, an oasis on the dead green plain, of long barrack-like buildings, garden-girt bungalows, and white tents. We had reached our journey's end. The church-bells were ringing as I rode into Quetta, for it was Sunday, and, unfortunately, a bright, fine morning. Had it been otherwise, I might have been spared the ordeal of riding, on a very dirty and attenuated camel, past a crowd of well-dressed women and frock-coated men on their way to church. As we passed a neat victoria, glistening with varnish, and drawn by a pair of good-looking, high-stepping ponies, containing a general in full uniform and a pretty, smartly dressed lady, I cast a glance behind me. Gerôme, who brought up the rear of the caravan, had (for coolness) divested himself of boots and socks, and, sublimely unconscious, was refreshing himself from the contents of a large wicker flask. One cannot, unfortunately, urge on a camel or quicken his pace at these awkward moments, and I passed a very uncomfortable quarter of an hour before reaching the Dák bungalow. But a glance at a looking-glass reassured me. No one would ever have taken the brick-coloured, ragged-looking ruffians we had become for Europeans.

I accepted a kind and courteous invitation from Mr. L——, of the Indo-European Telegraph, with pleasure, for the Dák bungalow was dirty and comfortless. Although my host and charming hostess would have made any place agreeable, Quetta is, from everything but a strategical point of view, dull and uninteresting. It is an English garrison town, and all is said. The usual nucleus of scandal, surrounded by dances, theatricals, polo, flirtation, drink, and—divorce. Are they not all alike from Gibraltar to Hong Kong?

Under the guidance of my host, however, a pleasant trip was made to the Khojak tunnel. When one considers the comparatively short time it has been in hand, it is almost incredible that, with so many difficulties (water, hard rock, etc.), this work should have progressed as it has. The tunnel, which runs due east and west, is, or will be, two miles and a half in length and three hundred and sixty-five feet in depth at the deepest part from the earth's surface. From the eastern end only sixty-five miles over a firm and level plain separates it from Kandahár. Even when I was there,[38] a light line could have been laid to that city in six weeks without difficulty. The plant, rails, and sleepers were on the spot, having been carried over the hill, and a railway-carriage could then run from Calcutta to the eastern extremity of the tunnel without break of gauge. The tunnel, when completed, will be thirty-four feet broad, and twenty-five feet in height.

A curious incident happened at one of the railway-stations between Quetta and Karachi. At the buffet of the one in question, I found Gerôme conversing volubly in Russian with a total stranger, a native. On inquiry I found he was a very

[38] April, 1889. The boring of the tunnel is now accomplished.

old friend, a Russian subject and native of Samarcand. "He has just come through from Cábul," said my companion. "He often does this journey"—ostensibly for purposes of trade.

The 20th of April saw us in Bombay. An Italian steamer, the *Venezia*, was leaving for the Black Sea direct, and in her I secured a passage for Gerôme, who was not impressed with our Eastern possessions. The crowd of curious natives who persistently followed him everywhere may have had something to do with it, for a fur-clad Esquimaux in Piccadilly would not have created a greater sensation than my companion in high boots, black velvet breeches, and red caftan in the busy streets of the great Indian city. Only a Russian could have existed in that blazing sun with no other protection to the head than the astrachan bonnet, which he obstinately refused to discard. I saw him safely on board, and something very like a tear came into my trusty little friend's eyes, as we shook hands and parted, to meet, perhaps, never again. For a better companion no man could wish. Plucky, honest as the day, and tender-hearted as a woman was Gerôme Realini; and it was with a feeling of loneliness and sincere regret that I watched the grey smoke of the *Venezia* sink below the blue waters, which were soon to bear me, also, back to England and European civilization.

Has the journey been worth it? Has the result repaid one for the cold, dirt, and privation of Persia, the torrid heat and long desert marches through Baluchistán? Perhaps not. There are some pleasant hours, however, to look back upon. Kashán, a vision of golden domes and dim, picturesque caravanserais; Ispahán, with its stately Madrassa and blue Zandarood, winding lazily through miles on miles of white and scarlet poppyland; Shiráz, a dream of fair women, poetry, and roses, in its setting of emerald plain, sweet-scented gardens, and cypress trees. These, at any rate, are bright oases in that somewhat dreary ride from Teherán to the sea. And then—nearing India—the quiet midday siesta after the hot dusty march; the *al fresco* repast by the light of a glorious sunset, and the welcome rest and fragrant pipe in the cool night air of the silent, starlit desert.

APPENDICES

APPENDIX A.

LIST OF STATIONS AND DISTANCES FROM RÉSHT TO BUSHIRE, PERSIA.

	English Miles.
Résht	—
Koudoum	20
Rustemabad	20
Menjil	12
Patchinar	8
Kharzán	16
Kazvin	24
Kavarek	16
Kishlak	16
Yengi-Imàm	16
Hessarek	16
Shahabad	16
Teherán	16
Rabat Kerim	28
Pitché	24
Kushku Baïra	16
Mahometabad	28
Koom	16
Pasingán	16
Sin-sin	28
Kashán	24
Khurood	28
Bideshk	24
Murchakhar	24

Géz	24
Ispahán	12
Djulfa	3
Marg	12
Mayar	24
Koomisháh	20
Magsogh-Beg	16
Yezdi-Ghazt	24
Shoulgistán	24
Abadéh	20
Sourmah	16
Khina-Khoreh	28
Deybid	20
Mourghab	28
Kawamabad	24
Sivánd	8
Poozeh	16
Zergoon	20
Shiráz	20
Chinar-Ráda	8
Khaneh Zinián	24
Dashti Arjin	12
Meyun Kotal	12
Kazeroon	20
Kamarij	24
Konar Takta	12
Dalaki	12
Borazjun	16
Sheif	28
	979
From Sheif to Bushire by sea	7
Total English miles	986

APPENDIX B.

ROUTE—SONMIANI TO QUETTA.

Halting-place.	English Miles.	Remarks.
Sonmiani		Small sea-port town. Water abundant, but brackish. Fodder and supplies procurable.
Shekh-Raj	18	Road fairly good. Water sweet and plentiful.
Outhal	14	Road stony and undulating; crossed dry bed of river Purali. Well of brackish water.
Shekron-ka-Got	22	Road sandy. Passed several salt marshes. No water.
Beïla	24	Road good through rich alluvial land irrigated by river Purali. Road near to Beïla intersected by deep nullahs distressing to camels. Water plentiful; supplies procurable.
Lakh	18	Road good and level till Pass of Lakh, which is steep and extremely difficult. Water usually procurable, though very brackish. Forage for horse and camel a mile distant.
Natchi	19	Road stony and difficult, through country irrigated (in wet season) by river Lakh. A small grazing ground midway, frequented by nomads. Water uncertain. Forage (for camel only) plentiful.
Lar-Anderi	20	Road along dry river bed about three hundred yards wide (name unknown), for about five miles. Then over Plain of Arrah, sparsely cultivated. At end of stage crossed river Lar-Anderi, a broad but shallow stream about sixty yards wide, seldom dry. Good water from river, but brackish from wells, of which there are three. Forage for horse and camel.
Jhow	14	Crossed Jhow and Seridab rivers, both dry. No cultivation to be seen. Water plentiful and sweet. Forage for horse and camel.

Noundra	20	Unexplored. No road. Travelling fairly easy. Water brackish.
Kanéro	about 20	Unexplored. Road rough and stony, overgrown in parts with scrub. A very narrow track extends from Noundra to Kanéro, which we followed. No water or forage.
Dhaïra	about 20	Unexplored. No road, but struck several narrow paths leading in all directions. Water plentiful and good. Forage for horse and camel.
Gwarjak	about 20	Unexplored. Road level and good. Water abundant, also forage for horse and camel, but natives unfriendly.
Gajjar	13	Road good, through cultivated country. Water good and plentiful. Forage for horse and camel procurable, also supplies.
Jebri	20	Road good, though deep and marshy in places. Water good and plentiful, also horse and camel forage.
Greshak	26	Road leads over the Barida Pass. Gradual and easy ascent and descent. Water good and plentiful. Forage for camel only.
Loch	18	Road very narrow and much overgrown (lost in places) with scrub. Water scarce. Forage scarce for camel, none for horse.
Gidar	32	Good and level road. Water procurable from river only. Forage for camel only.
Sohrab	26	Road difficult. Passed several steep, but not lofty, ranges of hills. Water plentiful, but brackish. No forage for horse or camel.
Rodingo	36	Road level and easy. Much camelthorn, wild thyme, and (English) furze on either side of track. Water good, but scarce. No forage for horse or camel.
Kelát	14	Road well defined, and level. Water good and abundant. Forage for horse and camel. Supplies of all kinds procurable.
Mangachar	26	Road well defined and level. Leads through a fertile country. Water good. Forage for horse and camel, and supplies procurable.

Mastung	32	Road level and good, but intersected by deep nullahs, rendering it difficult for heavily laden camels. Water good and plentiful. Forage for horse and camel, and supplies procurable.
Quetta	32	Road excellent, and in parts macadamized. A garrison town, and railway to all parts of India.
Total English miles	504	

APPENDIX C.

TABLE OF LANGUAGES OF NORTH AND SOUTH BALUCHISTÁN.

	Makrán (South).	Kalati (North).
Ant	Mor	Khar
Ashes	Pūr	Hiss
Barley	O	Sār
Boy	Bachak	Mār
Cold	Sara	Yakt
Copper	Rod	Miss
Day	Roch	Dēh
Dog	Kuchak	Kuchik
Earth	Duniah	Daghar
Fire	Ach	Khāka
Flower	Pūl	Pūl
Gold	Tila	Kisun
Heavy	Giran	Kolui
To eat	Warága	Kuning
To kill	Kushàja	Kasfing
To bring	Aràga	Atning
To see	Guidàga	Khanning

APPENDIX D.

TEMPERATURE (FAHRENHEIT) BETWEEN SONMIANI AND QUETTA, BALUCHISTÁN.

	Remarks.	Mid-day.	
		Shade.	Sun.
March			
16	Sonmiani. Fine; north-west breeze	79°	83°
17	Sonmiani. Fine; no breeze	73°	88°
18	Sonmiani. Fine; no breeze	72°	105°
19	Sonmiani. Fine; strong north-east breeze	80°	98°
20	Shekh-Raj. Fine; light north-east breeze	91°	118°
21	Outhal. Fine; light north-west breeze	92°	114°
22	Shekron-ka-Got. Fine; south-west breeze	93°	109°
23	Beïla. Rain and thunder; light south breeze	88°	92°
24	Beïla. Rain; no wind	83°	87°
25	Lakh. Fine; west wind	84°	103°
26	Natchi. Fine; light south-east breeze	91°	115°
27	Lar-Anderi. Dull; no breeze	93°	108°
28	Jhow. Fine; hot wind (north-east)	94°	110°
29	Noundra. Fine; hot south-west wind	96°	123°
30	Kanéro. Fine; south-west breeze	90°	120°
31	Dhaïra. Fine; light north breeze	95°	123°
April			
1	Gwarjak. Fine; light south-east breeze	91°	111°
2	Gajjar. Fine; south wind	93°	110°
3	Jebri. Fine; strong north-west wind	91°	110°
4	Greshak. Fine; strong north-west wind	85°	88°
5	Loch. Fine; strong north wind	76°	89°
6	Gidar. Fine; light south-east breeze	81°	86°

April			
7	Sohrab. Fine; light west breeze.	77°	86°
8	Dām. Rain; south-west wind	77°	78°
9	Kelát. Rain and dust storm	73°	75°
10	Kelát. Fine; west wind	59°	87°
11	Kelát. Fine; no breeze	58°	74°
12	Mangachar. Fine; no breeze	80°	95°
13	Mastung. Fine; hot wind.	89°	116°
14	Quetta. Dull; no breeze	64°	80°
15	Quetta. Fine; no breeze	61°	83°
16	Quetta. Fine; south-west breeze	63°	68°
17	Quetta. Fine; no breeze	65°	67°
18	Sukkur, Sind. A hot wind blowing	99°	117°

APPENDIX E.

GENEALOGY OF THE KHANS OF KELÁT.

- Kambar Khan.
  - Sambar.
    - Mahammad Khan.
      - Abdulla Khan.
        - Mobat Khan, reigned some time at Kelát; superseded by his brother, Nazir Khan, and died a hostage at Kandahár.
          - Haji Khan, died a hostage at Kandahár.
            - Baram Khan, died at Kelát
              - Ahmad Yar Khan, slain by Mehrab Khan.
        - Eltarz Khan, slain accidentally by his brother, Nazir Khan.
        - Nazir Khan, originally a hostage at Kandahár; superseded his brother, Mobat Khan, and reigned forty years.
          - Mahmud Khan, reigned at Kelát.
            - Mehrab han, slain by the British troops.
              - Hassan Khan (poisoned).
              - Khudadad Khan, present Ruler.
            - Azem Khan.
          - Mohamed Rehim Khan, slain by sister of Mustapha Khan.
          - Mustapha Khan, slain by his brother, Mohamed Rehim Khan.
            - Sarafrez Khan, slain by Mehrab Khan.

MAP

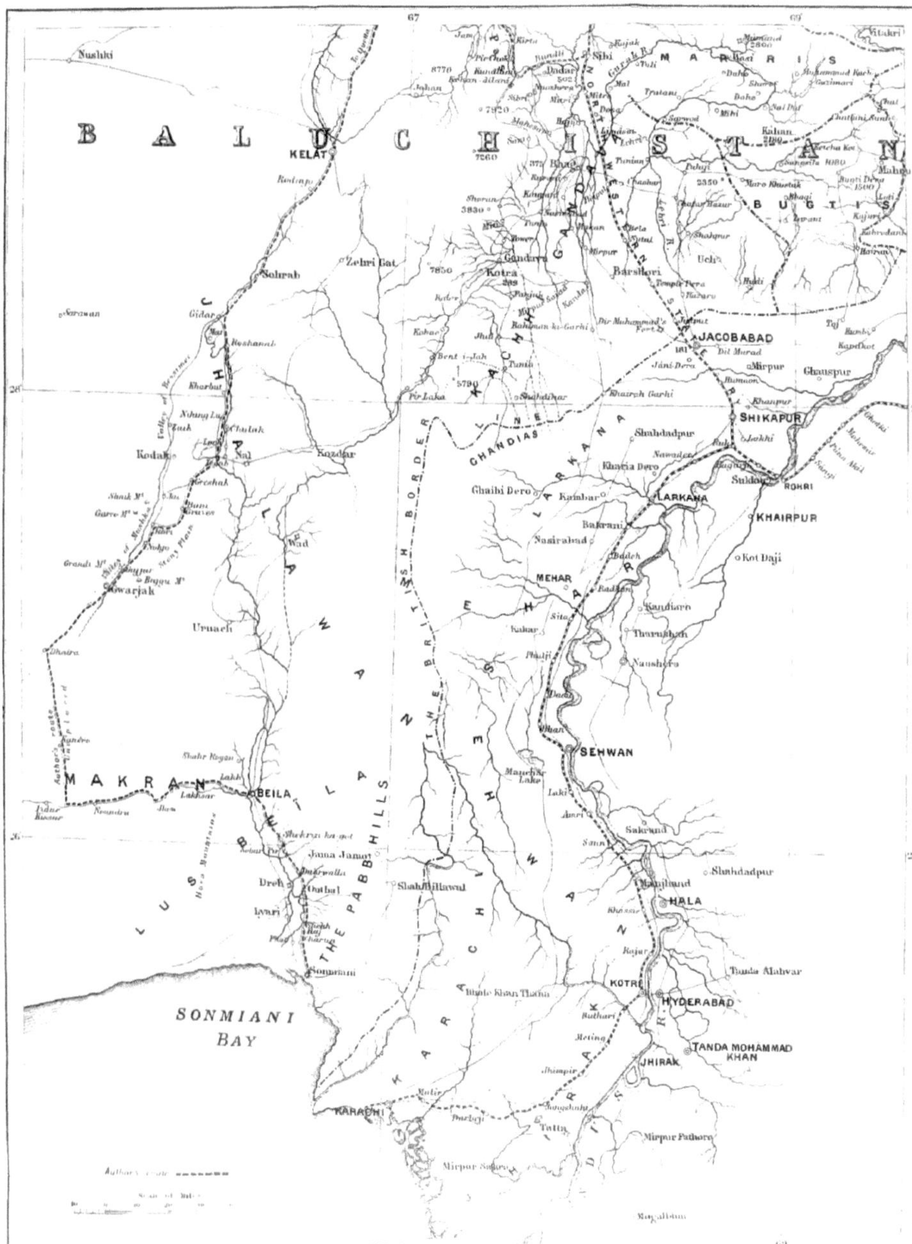

B A L U C H I S T A N
KELAT
Nushki
Sohrab
Zehri Bat
Kozdar
Kodak
Nal
Wad
Awarjak
Urnach
Sibi
Dadar
Gandava
Kotra
Jhal
M A R R I S
B U G T I S
JACOBABAD
SHIKAPUR
Ghauspur
ROHRI
Sukkur
KHAIRPUR
Kot Daji
LARKANA
Kambar
Ghaibi Dero
Nasirabad
MEHAR
CHANDIAS
LINE
THE BRITISH BORDER
M A K R A N
BEILA
SEHWAN
Manchhar Lake
Sakrand
Shahdadpur
HALA
KOTRI
HYDERABAD
TANDA MOHAMMAD KHAN
JHIRAK
Tatta
Mirpur Sakro
Mirpur Pathoro
SONMIANI BAY
Sonmiani
KARACHI
THE PABB HILLS
SHAHBANDAR

MAP

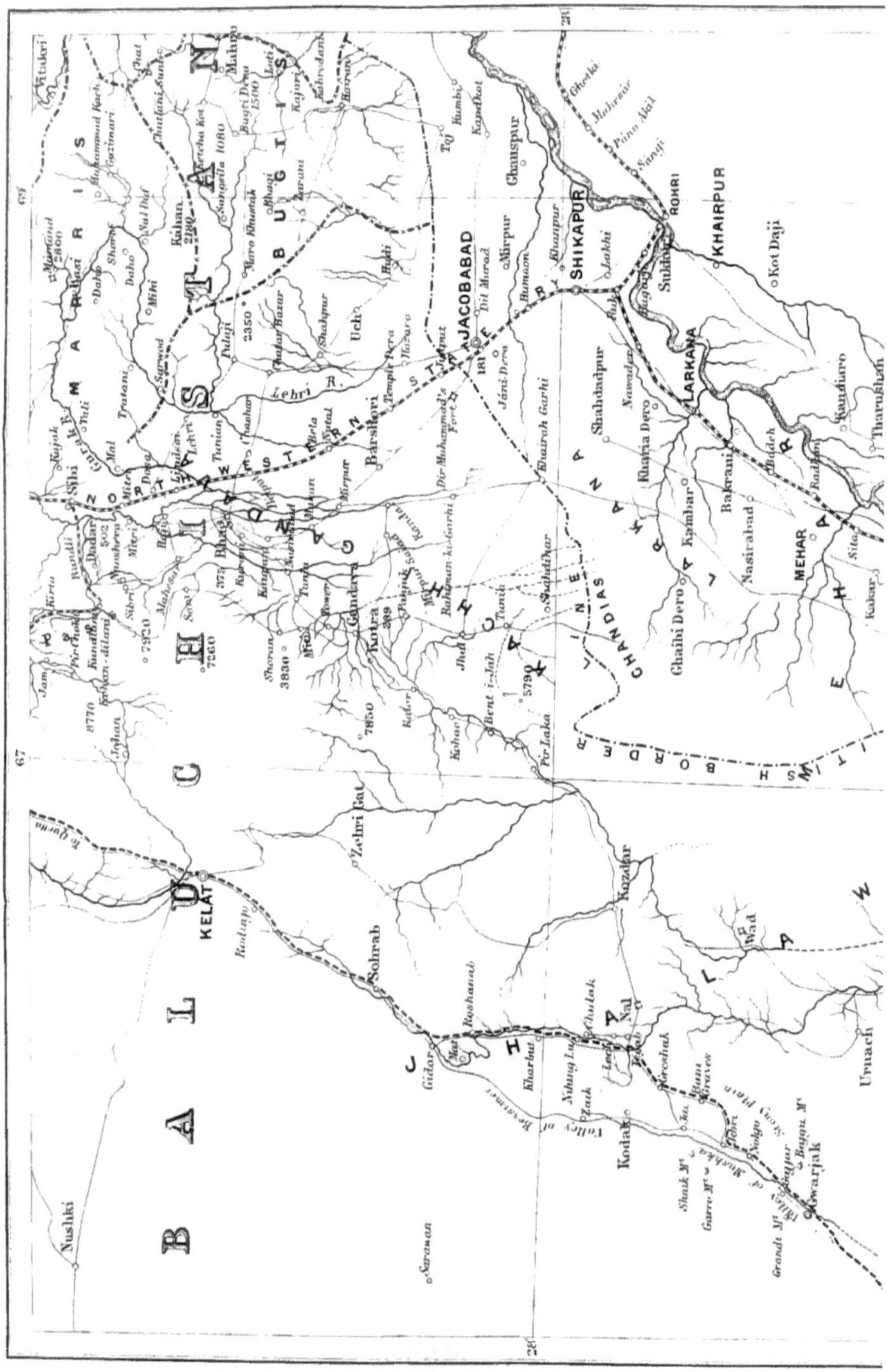

Map (*Enlarged - Top*)

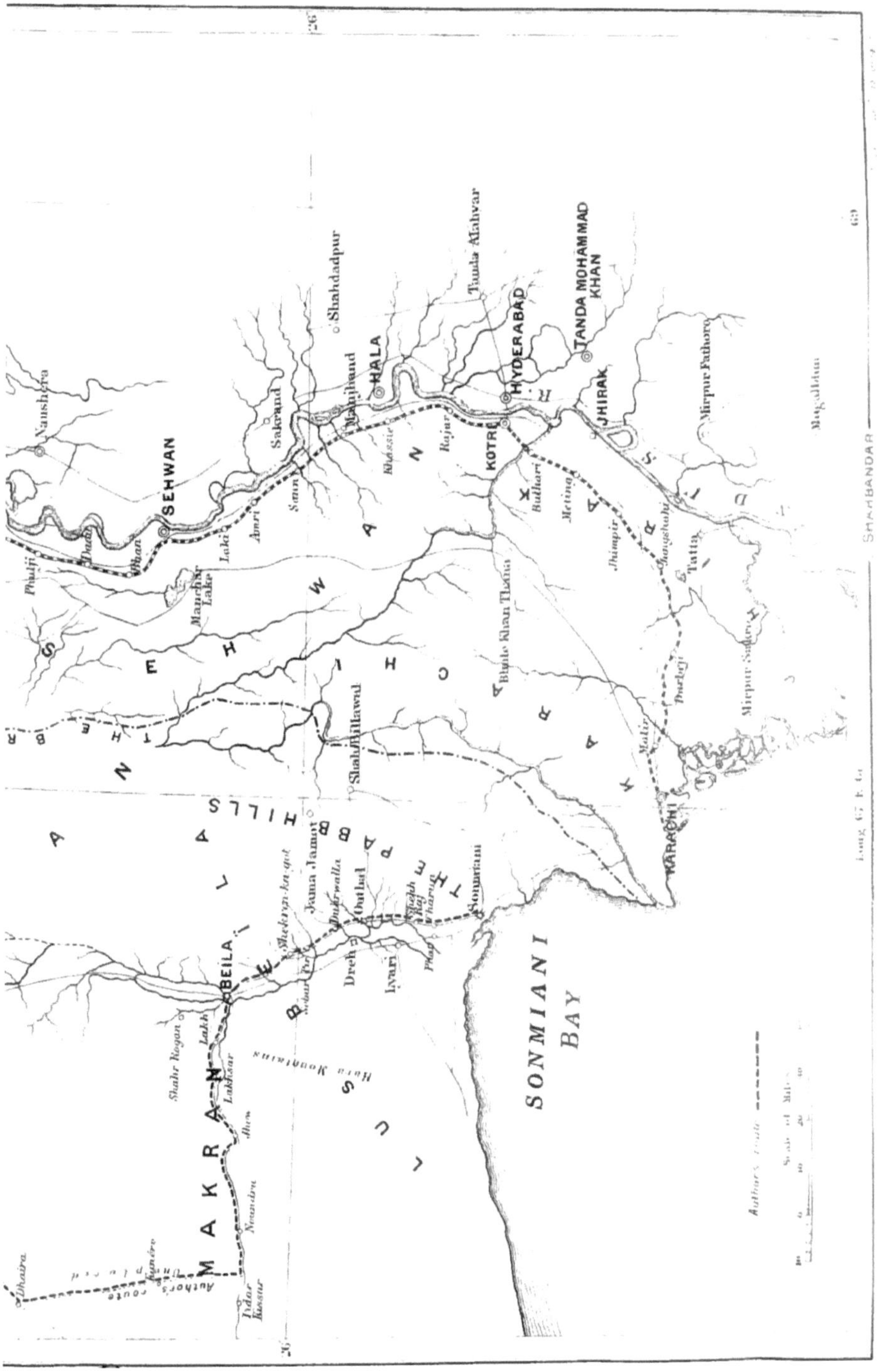

Map (*Enlarged - Bottom*)

Printed by Libri Plureos GmbH in Hamburg,
Germany

9 789358 007794